The Active Mentor

D0117641

*This book is dedicated to everyone who takes the time to assist,
encourage, and support new teachers.*

The Active Mentor

Practical Strategies for Supporting New Teachers

Ron Nash

Foreword by
Kay Burke

CORWIN
A SAGE Company

Copyright © 2010 by Corwin

All rights reserved. When forms and sample documents are included, their use is authorized only by educators, local school sites, and/or noncommercial or nonprofit entities that have purchased the book. Except for that usage, no part of this book may be reproduced or utilized in any form or by any means, electronic or mechanical, including photocopying, recording, or by any information storage and retrieval system, without permission in writing from the publisher.

For information:

Corwin
A SAGE Company
2455 Teller Road
Thousand Oaks, California 91320
(800) 233-9936
Fax: (800) 417-2466
www.corwinpress.com

SAGE Ltd.
1 Oliver's Yard
55 City Road
London EC1Y 1SP
United Kingdom

SAGE Pvt. Ltd.
B 1/I 1 Mohan Cooperative
   Industrial Area
Mathura Road, New Delhi 110 044
India

SAGE Asia-Pacific Pte. Ltd.
33 Pekin Street #02-01
Far East Square
Singapore 048763

Printed in the United States of America

Library of Congress Cataloging-in-Publication Data

Nash, Ron, 1949-
The active mentor: practical strategies for supporting new teachers/Ron Nash; foreword by Kay Burke.
      p. cm.
Includes bibliographical references and index.
ISBN 978-1-4129-8050-0 (pbk.)

   1. First year teachers—United States. 2. Mentoring in education—United States. I. Title.

LB2844.1.N4N36 2010
371.102—dc22   2009047378

This book is printed on acid-free paper.

09   10   11   12   13   10 9 8 7 6 5 4 3 2 1

Acquisitions Editor:	Hudson Perigo
Associate Editor:	Julie McNall
Production Editor:	Veronica Stapleton
Copy Editor:	Adam Dunham
Typesetter:	C&M Digitals (P) Ltd.
Proofreader:	Charlotte Waisner
Indexer:	Sheila Bodell
Cover Designer:	Karine Hovsepian

Contents

Foreword

V eteran teachers and administrators who read *The Active Mentor* will reflect on their first years of teaching and wish they could have had Ron Nash as their mentor. Ron's love of teaching, understanding of human nature, and ability to know what beginning teachers need to be successful make him the quintessential mentor and an authentic author. Novice teachers may not be able to experience Ron's personal mentoring expertise in their own classrooms, but they can experience his written wisdom and practical advice by reading this book. A few overlooked details could cause first-year teachers anxiety and confusion the first week of school. Ron Nash weaves storytelling and realistic dialogue to set the stage for what mentors should model for new teachers to help them gain the confidence they need to start the school year. He describes the importance of creating the positive classroom climate that fosters cooperation, respect, and active engagement that are critical for success in teaching.

I was amazed at the number of vivid memories I recalled about my first year of teaching after Ron described his own early teaching experiences. It certainly takes more than knowledge of the subject matter to succeed in education. Often, our success depends on the "kindness of strangers" embodied by both informal and formal mentors who shape our "style" of teaching and allow us to survive that critical first year of teaching. The first year often determines whether or not we succeed in our chosen profession or if we become the "one out of three teachers" who end up leaving the profession within the first few years. Recently, I met with two teacher friends who became my informal mentors when I began my teaching career at Stranahan High School in Broward County, Florida, in 1970. We arrived at school at 10 a.m. each day and planned until noon. Since we were overcrowded and on split sessions, we new teachers were the "second shift" who taught for five straight hours from noon to five. The school was not air-conditioned, so we would turn off the noisy oscillating fans when we lectured and then turn them on again when the students did the work. Anyone who has visited South Florida in September has experienced the excessive heat and humidity. Imagine being jammed in a classroom with 35 sweaty ninth graders studying participles, gerunds, and infinitives. Our school did not have a formal mentor program, but Diane DeFelice and Karen Owen taught similar classes and the two-hour planning time we shared each morning was invaluable to me. They gave me copies of worksheets, lesson plans, and tests; and most important, they shared organization and behavior management techniques. Wearing my long hair in a neat bun made me look older than my 22 years, but I always felt green and those students could sense it. If it were not for Diane and Karen's informal mentoring, I truly believe I would have quit teaching during my first year.

The Active Mentor should be required reading for all administrators, mentors, coaches, teachers, and professional developers. Ron's advice and strategies are both practical and profound. Even if schools cannot afford a formal teacher induction program and have no funds to pay and train mentors, this book could be used in a study group or as professional reading to begin the conversations before school starts. Ron's emphasis on proactive preparation for the first week of school and on interactive instruction throughout the year is artfully delivered through vignettes. The realistic interactions and dialogue between the novice teacher, the mentors, and the administrators in the stories help identify how schools should establish a mentoring program that incorporates so many of the practical and useful tactics described in the book. In today's economic environment, the importance of a quality education delivered by highly effective teachers has never been more important. It is imperative that we attract, train, and retain effective teachers. Ron Nash offers an inexpensive and practical program for mentors and novice teachers that will ensure success for teachers and ultimately for the students they teach. *The Active Mentor* could serve as a textbook for preservice, graduate, and inservice training as well as a handbook for beginning teachers, veteran teachers, mentors, administrators, and professional developers whose common goal is to improve teaching and learning. If teachers are not fortunate enough to have Ron Nash as their personal mentor, they can at least have this book to guide and support them, as they become successful educators in the 21st century.

Kay Burke

Preface

Obstacles to success have a habit of presenting themselves early in the career of every teacher. Even novice teachers are veteran students, and as such they are often capable of inferring from their own experiences exactly what obstacles will need to be dealt with, sidestepped, or otherwise overcome on the way to a successful first year in the profession. Other impediments to success may come as a surprise, and on occasion they come not in single spies, but in battalions. However and whenever they come, the question for every teacher is this: How much frustration can she take before she decides the resultant pain is not worth the effort?

New teachers, of course, react to challenges differently. Yost (2006) affirms that "some teachers are both resilient and persistent, remaining in the profession despite being confronted with the same challenges and obstacles of those who leave" (p. 59). But there are those who leave, and those who leave are departing in droves. Yost cites figures from the 2004 National Center for Educational Statistics that estimate that one-third of teachers leave the profession within three years (p. 59). Estimates may differ by a few percentage points, and in urban schools the rate is higher, but the sad truth is that *teacher retention is a significant problem in the United States.*

Obstacles are part of teaching, as they are part of life. The sheer size, number, and scope of these challenges can short-circuit an otherwise productive and satisfying teaching career in its infancy. Bobek (2001) lists an ability to solve problems as one of five factors keeping teachers in the classroom. In fact, there are many thousands of new teachers who, left on their own, will work their way through even the most difficult challenges that confront them on a daily basis; there are many thousands more who, when faced with myriad obstacles in the schoolhouse, will simply make the decision to walk away from a profession they once believed held great promise.

Still others, unwilling to give up on teaching, give up on a particular school environment that is not supportive or conducive to learning, and search "for schools that [make] good teaching possible" (Johnson & Birkeland, 2003, p. 21). Those teachers simply leave a bad environment for a better one. For teachers who are persistent and determined to succeed, shifting from one school to another voluntarily can be refreshing and reinvigorating.

The truth is that the obstacles encountered by new teachers may seem new and surprising to them, but such obstacles are not new to the profession. In working with teacher mentors over the years, a colleague and I often asked them what problems are faced by new teachers, and we made an extensive list. Not surprisingly, even though we were brainstorming with new groups of mentors each time, the lists looked the same. Classroom management, process management, discipline, dealing with parents, and other timeless (and time-related) issues always made the list. Teacher preparation and teacher induction programs (including a mentoring component) should prepare prospective teachers and new hires for what we know lies ahead. If the system is hemorrhaging teachers at the rate of one in three every three years then the system is in need of some attention and a great deal of repair.

Mentoring new teachers should involve helping them anticipate, understand, and overcome obstacles to success in the classroom. Too many teachers are left in isolation to try and figure all this out on their own. As a new teacher, my mentor encouraged me to "call him if I had questions," and informed me that "his door was always open." Unfortunately, I did not even know enough about teaching to know which questions were worthy of taking the time to knock on his door. Any support system worthy of the name helps teachers surface questions, answering some and, more important, equipping them to come up with ways to solve their own problems.

Helping new teachers understand a mandatory lesson-plan format requires a bit of modeling, and is easily accomplished in a short period of time. On the other hand, getting new teachers to understand what to do when a student talks back or is highly disruptive requires more reflection and a much deeper conversation about how the brain works in moments of high stress. I might have asked my mentor about the lesson-plan format, but I would have balked at approaching him about backtalk or disruptions. I simply did not know him well enough to open up on sensitive issues that might reveal my own shortcomings or lack of knowledge and experience.

In the absence of a real mentor-protégé relationship, a teacher is likely to find answers only after a confrontation with a student has led to a good deal of emotional discomfort and some real doubts about whether or not the situation was correctly handled. The sad thing is that everyone in education understands that such confrontations will come, yet we may do little to prepare the new teacher for that eventuality and the pain it causes. A teacher who is handed the room key and told to "hang in there" is quite likely headed for trouble not too far down the road. Teachers who are left to operate in relative isolation with little support may find themselves taking a "whack-a-mole" approach to problem solving.

The cost of not serving the needs of new teachers is high, and not only in human terms. Portner (2005b) cites a 2004 Alliance for Excellent Education report that estimates that $2.6 billion is spent annually in this country replacing teachers who have left the profession (p. xxi). That same report affirmed that "only 1 percent of beginning teachers currently receive the ongoing training and support that constitutes comprehensive induction when they enter the teaching profession" (p. xxii). Researchers, according to Portner,

> reinforced what had already become evident to practitioners: When these programs were well designed and implemented, novice teachers were not only staying longer; they were also developing into better teachers—and doing so at a faster rate—than had many before them. (p. xxii)

There can be little doubt that new teachers need substantive support so that they can avoid becoming casualties. We need to simultaneously reduce the teacher attrition rate and serve the needs of 21st-century students who have been essentially rewired by technology, suffused with information, and presented with obstacles of their own. If the role of the teacher is essential in facilitating the progress of students today, then the teacher support system must be up to the task. Schools and school districts need to commit to providing the kind of systemic support that will reduce obstacles and assist teachers in dealing with those that arise during the first two or three years of teaching. Effective schools build leadership capacity and interdependency by developing a collaborative structure within which new *and* veteran teachers feel safe, supported, and valued.

Below are descriptions of the eight chapters of this book, arranged in what I trust is a logical sequence:

Chapter 1: The Need for Heroes

If we as humans often have a need for heroes, for teachers that role is often filled by other teachers from our past who possessed various basic principles that were apparent right away or perhaps later, when we took the time to reflect on what defines such greatness. In this first chapter, I have identified and elaborated upon nine qualities highly effective teachers demonstrate on a daily basis.

Chapter 2: The Need for Speed

As we have seen, too many teachers leave the profession all too soon. They work against strong headwinds and encounter seemingly innumerable obstacles until they just turn in their keys, pack their belongings in a box, and leave the profession they had always thought would be their life's work. Teachers leave for many reasons, not the least of which is a lack of support on the part of administrators and colleagues in schools where isolationism has become a well-established fact of school life. In this chapter, we'll examine the need to create more support in order to stem the flow of teachers out of the profession.

Chapter 3: Clarity and Substance

Given the need for induction programs that provide new teachers with the support they need, how does mentoring fit into that system? Who should be a mentor? What, exactly, is the task of the teacher mentor? This chapter will explore the role of the teacher mentor in facilitating the continuous-improvement journey of new teachers in the schoolhouse.

Chapter 4: Ramping Up Relationships

A mentor who teaches the same subject as his protégé needs to know more than his subject area. Building a solid and productive professional relationship with the new teacher is critical if the pairing is going to click. In this chapter, we'll look at the inner workings of a successfully developed relationship. The kind of reflective conversations that will help mentors and protégés come together with a shared vision are possible only in strong relationships where trust and respect are mutual.

Chapter 5: A Place for Everything

Once the relationship-building process is underway, mentors and protégés need to set aside time during the summer to plan for the fall. My sense is that one reason new teachers have problems is that they enter the school year simply reacting to events. Someone—too often a well-meaning mentor—hands the new teacher a curriculum guide, the teacher's edition of the textbook, the keys to their class-room, and a class list and locker assignments—and encourages the new teacher to call if she has questions. The teacher subsequently heads into the school year with this logistical checklist completed and totally unaware of what is going to happen when 120 seventh-graders—veteran students all—descend on her over the course of four class periods. In this chapter, we'll suggest some ways to put the process horse before the content cart.

Chapter 6: Everything in Its Place

The focus of every teacher ought to be instruction. Once teachers have procedures, rules, and routines established—and understood—by students, it is time to facilitate the learning process in a way that gets results. In this chapter, we will suggest that the essence of powerful and effective teaching is to get the students to do the work. Too many kids come to school to watch teachers lecture, entertain, and generally do most of the work themselves. We'll explore ways mentors can help their protégés shift the workload from themselves to the students.

Chapter 7: When Good Gets Better

Induction programs need to stress continuous improvement on the part of everyone in the building. No one—no matter how senior—is at the stage where improvement is not possible. Mentors working with new teachers can help them establish a system for improvement that is self-sustaining. Administrators need to model this systemic improvement by creating a professional learning community dedicated to helping Eddie do tomorrow what he could not do today.

In this chapter, we'll explain how goals and benchmarks are critical signposts on the continuous-improvement journey of new teachers and, not coincidentally, students.

Chapter 8: Perspiration and Inspiration

New teachers work incredibly hard in an environment unfamiliar to them, but hard work is not enough to ensure success. Administrators, mentors, and colleagues need to be enlisted in the cause of keeping new teachers functioning effectively throughout the course of that first year. Before and during that first 180 days, new teachers should see great teachers in action, and they should be challenged by mentors and inspired by principals and colleagues dedicated to their success. A new teacher looking back on a rewarding first year may credit many heroes with providing the inspiration that in part at least helped them make progress while keeping their sanity. In our pursuit of excellence using diagnostic tools, instructional strategies, data analysis, and effective assessment techniques, we should not underestimate the power and influence of inspiration.

In the Prologue, we'll continue a story begun in my second book, *The Active Teacher* (2010), with a visit to a fictional middle school where the main—and wholly fictional—characters are Mr. Crandall, the school's principal; Trey, now a veteran teacher and outstanding teacher mentor; and Shellie, a new social studies teacher on the Cardinal team. Throughout the book, we'll call on this supporting cast in order to emphasize a point or provide context.

Acknowledgments

While working as an organizational development specialist with the Virginia Beach City Public Schools, I had the pleasure of training mentors alongside Karen O'Meara, at that time the coordinator of the district's mentor program. I also spent two years as the director of what we called TOCLI (Teacher Orientation and Continuous Learning Institute). This weeklong institute was the first part of our new teacher induction program, and working with those new teachers and assisting in the training of teacher mentors was an absolute pleasure. The experience made me realize how important mentors are to novice teachers, and I thank Karen O'Meara for being a great mentor program coordinator and training partner.

Once again, I owe a debt of gratitude to Hudson Perigo, my editor, along with a great supporting cast at Corwin Press. As this book is about mentoring, I must acknowledge three wonderful educators and authors who have inspired me over the years. Dr. Rich Allen wrote the foreword to my first book, *The Active Classroom*. Dr. Fred Jones did the honors for *The Active Teacher*, and Dr. Kay Burke contributed the foreword for this book. Each of these three wonderful professionals continues to inspire me, and I am forever grateful for their support and their dedication to teaching and learning.

As always, I thank my wife, Candy, for her support of my pursuit of a rather late-in-the-game career as full-time presenter and author.

About the Author

Ron Nash is the author of the Corwin bestseller *The Active Classroom* (2008), a book dedicated to shifting students from passive observers to active participants in their own learning. Ron's professional career in education has included teaching social studies at the middle and high school levels. He also served as an instructional coordinator and organizational development specialist for the Virginia Beach City Public Schools for 13 years. In that capacity, Ron trained thousands of teachers and other school division employees in such varied topics as classroom management, instructional strategies, presentation techniques, relationship building, customer service, and process management. After Ron's retirement from the Virginia Beach City Public Schools in 2007, he founded Ron Nash and Associates, Inc., a company dedicated to working with teachers in the area of brain-compatible learning. Originally from Pennsylvania, Ron and his wife, Candy, a French teacher, have lived in Virginia Beach for the past 24 years. Ron can be reached through his Web site at www.ronnashand associates.com.

Prologue

Trey's principal, Mr. Crandall, informed him on May 18th that Shellie, a newly graduated teacher from a local college, had been hired as a replacement for a departing seventh-grade social studies teacher on the Cardinal team. Mr. Crandall invited Trey to a meeting with Shellie on May 20th, and Trey's job from that meeting on would be to begin the process of facilitating Shellie's growth as a teacher for the next two years. In a careful hiring process, Mr. Crandall and the members of the Cardinal team had been impressed by Shellie's attitude and demeanor. Having brought her on board, her new Cardinal teammates, Trey, and Mr. Crandall were committed to her success.

Trey would be her official mentor, but new teachers in their middle school did not suffer from a lack of attention. From the media specialist in the library to the computer resource teachers to the custodians, everyone in the building had a supporting role in assisting Shellie and three other new teachers. It was not always the case that teachers were hired before school was out, but the induction system Mr. Crandall had developed over his many years as principal took advantage of her early hire to begin the process of acclimating Shellie to her new surroundings. Trey also taught social studies, and whenever possible Mr. Crandall provided new teachers with someone who taught the same subject.

Trey had come to the middle school ten years ago, and his decade-long tenure here stood in marked contrast to his first year of teaching in another school, where "hang in there" seemed to have been the extent of the support program. His move to this school was born of frustration, along with a desire to teach United States history. As a member of the Phoenix team, Trey had been mentored by Mrs. Slattery, an outstanding English teacher who had since retired. Although there had been some attrition on the Phoenix team over the years, their support system never wavered. Trey and his teammates knew that teacher isolation, especially in a team-teaching situation, was simply not an option. Those who had left, like Mrs. Slattery, did so due to retirement or factors unrelated to job satisfaction.

The principal, Mr. Crandall, had built a great deal of leadership capacity at the school, and any teacher mentor had at his or her disposal a wide range of talent on staff—talent that came in handy when new teachers joined the faculty. For instance, several teachers who were famously and highly analytical worked with new teachers on establishing processes in the classroom. Those analytical teachers tended to ask a great many more questions than others on the faculty, and they had the patience to work with new teachers to develop processes related to managing the classroom—things like establishing consistencies in the returning of tests, providing feedback on assignments, and what norms to use when getting the attention of students. In a building that valued people for their individual talents and strengths, new teachers could count on a great deal of support from many directions.

Very quickly, Trey arranged for Shellie to observe two excellent social studies teachers in the building. Before her visits, Trey told her to watch the students—not the teacher—and answer three basic questions while in the classrooms: (1) Did the students appear to be fully engaged? (2) Who appeared to be doing the most work, teacher or students? and (3) What message did the students' nonverbal language convey? The two observations took place over the course of three days. After school on the third day, Trey met with Shellie to see what she had noticed. Using the three questions as starting points, Trey facilitated a reflective conversation that ended up with a discussion about various learning environments. Trey explained that new teachers have thousands of hours of classroom experience as students, and he gently probed with questions about various learning styles, her own included.

Trey's purpose in having Shellie observe these quality teachers while concentrating on the students in those classrooms was to allow her to compare and contrast what she had observed with her own experiences as a student. Shellie admitted that she had experienced few classroom experiences where she—and not the teacher—did most of the work. Comparing and contrasting her own experiences with what she had seen resulted in a commitment on her part to make sure she truly involved students in their own learning. In the course of this mentor-protégé conversation, Trey did not actually *tell* Shellie anything, nor did he give her any particular advice. He let her come to her own conclusions based on what she had seen and heard, combined with her own rich experience in the educational system—an experience that included thirteen years in K–12 and an additional four years of college. *Her classroom observations and her own past combined to provide rich context for a reflective conversation.*

Another of Trey's immediate tasks was to bring Shellie and her support system together as soon as possible in the summer. One of the members of the Cardinal team had provided Trey with several summer days on which Shellie could meet with the entire team and do some preliminary planning for the school year. This was accomplished in an informal setting—usually the house of a member of the team involved—and included a meal, along with some valuable relationship building. Trey still remembered his first year of teaching and the teammates he did not even meet until the week the teachers returned to school. They had been so absorbed in their own worlds that he was left to fend for himself. Shellie would find a team and a school ready to make her part of the family, a system years in the making and improved with the passing of each school year by Mr. Crandall and his leadership team.

Trey knew that by the time the teachers came back to school the week before students reported, Shellie would have already begun to form some powerful professional relationships. She would be invited to meet with the other social studies teachers in the school's professional-development library for a day in the summer, where she could get to know, along with a new sixth-grade social studies teacher, a bit more about the curriculum and resource materials available for her use.

Mr. Crandall invited all four new teachers to a picnic lunch at the school, and used that opportunity to stress the importance of the first week of school with students as a time to stress process—not content. His purpose was to impress on them that managing the classroom successfully demands that sufficient time be devoted to turning procedures into effective routines. Teachers can be headed for trouble if they introduce content before students know what it means to have a meaningful and effective conversation with another student, to brainstorm information so that everyone has input, to develop good listening skills, or to understand the reasons behind class rules and procedures. Mr. Crandall explained that classroom management is a frontloaded process that establishes an environment where students feel safe and will voluntarily share and discuss information on their way to creating knowledge. He pointed out that building relationships with students and their parents should be done early, in order to establish a relationship bank of sorts, where deposits can be made against the day when withdrawals are necessary.

By the time Shellie got to school for the mandatory week of inservice, she had met and gotten to know her own teammates, all the other new teachers, the principal and assistant principal, and several other members of the school staff. She knew what was expected of her during that first week with students, and she was beginning to feel at home. She had her classroom arranged as soon as the custodians finished her hallway so that when she reported to the school district's New Teacher Orientation prior to that school inservice week, she felt good about the choice she had made. Her room was ready, she had direction, and she had a support system in the schoolhouse that made her feel more confident about what lay ahead. She understood she was not yet truly competent, but she felt as ready as she could be to work with four classes of seventh-grade students.

Shellie became part of a collaborative school environment where the principal, Mr. Crandall, insisted on a continuous-improvement effort that precluded isolationist tendencies and encouraged lifelong learning in pursuit of excellence. He backed this up by viewing teacher workdays as opportunities for reflection and professional growth. On one Wednesday afternoon per month, students were dismissed early and once again teachers spent the time taking a close look at *how* they did *what* they did. District money was available for teachers weak in their subject area to take college courses in order to strengthen content knowledge. Mr. Crandall was relentless in the creation and maintenance of a school-level system that supported not just new teachers but veterans and support staff as well.

In Trey's previous school, the week teachers returned for inservice was divided between faculty meetings that amounted to info dumps on policy, insurance, and other "administrivia" and time for teachers to work in their classrooms. At this school, Mr. Crandall relegated all policy pronouncements to e-mails and information placed in teacher mailboxes during that first week back. Collaboration among teams, with the faculty as a whole, and between mentors and protégés was the norm. Trey met with Shellie, and explained that he would work with her on everything but subject-area content. The school district employed a series of content coaches who would work with her on matters related directly to the social studies curriculum. Opportunities would be made available for Shellie to observe classes within the building and elsewhere in the district. The teachers she would observe were part of the induction program, and time would be made available to have follow-up conversations with them. Trey pointed out that Mr. Crandall provided substitutes or class covers for such occasions.

Trey also explained to Shellie that while summative evaluations were required by the district, Mr. Crandall relied heavily on formative feedback provided by everyone, including himself, who would observe her in the classroom. One second-year teacher and another who had just completed her third year met with Shellie to confirm that the emphasis was on coaching, with its attendant and useful feedback, rather than on summative evaluations. These two teachers explained that Shellie would find plenty of assistance from the school administrators, teachers, and staff during her first couple of years. Coaches from the district level would, they said, be working with her during the course of the first year in a support—and not an evaluative—capacity. Summative evaluations were required, of course, but they came not out of the blue, but as a natural extension of the formative process.

Finally, early in that first week for teachers, Trey pulled together the four new teachers and explained the importance of process.

"There are principals who will encourage teachers to jump directly into the course content on the very first day with students," said Trey. "Mr. Crandall is not one of them. He is a proponent of putting the process horse before the content cart."

"What do you mean, exactly?" said Shellie.

"Teachers—veteran or otherwise—who ignore procedures and other process-related components of management may well find themselves in a deep hole several weeks into the school year. Students need to understand the processes established in your classroom to the extent that those processes become routine."

"I think I get that," said one of the new teachers. "Can you give us an example?"

"Sure," said Trey. "Every teacher on the planet has a way of getting the attention of students who are talking or otherwise engaged. In my classroom, I combine raising my hand with a verbal, 'Pause . . . look this way please.' I have found this combination of a visual and verbal cue to be very effective. It is effective in part because I practice 'bringing them back' dozens of time during the first week of school. I even use the sweep hand of my watch to gauge the amount of time it takes to bring them back, and we work at reducing that time span."

"Seems simple," said Shellie.

"It is simple, and it is effective if the procedure becomes routine, so that no matter what they are doing, using it brings them back. Many teachers will use half a dozen different cues on various occasions, something that students find confusing. Make it simple, practice it until it becomes routine, and getting their attention will happen as a matter of course."

One of the new teachers said, "At the district-wide orientation program, our team leaders worked with us a good deal on process management. We made a list of procedures like handing in homework and having a routine when students enter the room that provides continuity and gets them engaged quickly."

"Absolutely," said Trey. "Can you think of some others from the lists you compiled at the orientation workshops?"

Shellie said, "How about the procedure for sharpening a pencil?"

"Right again," said Trey, "along with getting ready for a chemistry lab and cleaning up in preparation for leaving at the end. Also, students in this school are used to having student-to-student discussions about content; they learn to explain and defend a point of view; this is new to many kids who perhaps have been used to sitting passively, watching teachers work, or gazing at videos or doing worksheets. The point here is that the first week of school can be spent creating a well-oiled machine where students understand the procedures and rules in such a way that once you get into course content, there will be little or no confusion about process. Believe me, spending five days getting your procedural house in order is well worth the effort. The team that ran the district orientation program put the emphasis in the right place—process."

Shellie's first year had its ups and downs, and there were times when she wished her college's teacher preparation program had been more complete and relevant, but by April she was certain that another year was in order. She received so much formative feedback during the course of the school year that the summative evaluation at year's end was decidedly anticlimactic. The school's support system was geared to working with new teachers in each of the four areas covered by the summative evaluation document, so nothing came as a surprise. Trey had helped her overcome obstacles by anticipating with her what they might be, and by developing in her a propensity for problem solving, in which she was helped by more analytical members of the staff who seemed to ask a million questions, but who ultimately assisted her in dealing with challenges that might have sunk her had she been entirely on her own.

Shellie's college roommate had also gone into teaching, but had a very different experience. She received no support from her administration or her fellow teachers. Problems multiplied, and she began to flounder in November, deciding in May that she would not return to teaching. Shellie tried to convince her to simply go to a different school and give it another shot, but her friend was convinced teaching was simply not for her. She took a job as a receptionist for a doctor who happened to be a family friend. Shellie spent a good deal of time reflecting on the contrast between what she and her college roommate had experienced, and she came to the conclusion that she was lucky to be in a school and school district where induction and mentoring were more than just words. Her two full weeks of district- and school-level preparation had helped tremendously, and she had spent the first week with students introducing and then honing procedures, and she had led her students in a long reflective conversation about ground rules for the classroom. She decided to let them use their own experience as students to surface behaviors that would facilitate process management throughout the year. During that first week, she combined the input from four classes into one set of five basic guidelines.

By the time she had hit the ground running with content on the sixth day of school, she and her students had been well prepared in terms of process. Her basic procedures had become routine, and students seemed to understand what was expected of them. They also understood what they could expect from her. Shellie considered that her time had been well spent during that first week, and while she was not sure she felt in any way competent, she went into her second week with students with increasing confidence. The incredible induction system at her middle school contributed in no small measure to Shellie's initial success.

Introduction

This book is for teacher mentors, teachers who are thinking of becoming mentors, and for administrators who seek to put in place a mentor program that will assist new teachers with their professional growth. I believe school cultures that reflect a collaborative approach to continuous improvement and professional development will provide much more natural support for teacher mentors than cultures where isolationism is the rule. While I don't claim to provide a step-by-step approach to setting up a school-level induction system, I do lend support to the idea that mentors trying to assist new teachers need support themselves; indeed everyone in the schoolhouse ought to be dedicated to assisting new teachers and accelerating their continuous-improvement journey.

In this book, I have followed the lead of others who use the term *protégé* for the teacher with whom the mentor is working. That protégé may be a novice teacher or one with experience who is new to the school. Over the past 15 years I have worked with thousands of new and veteran teachers, teacher mentors, and substitute teachers. Helping to train these wonderful people was a part of my work as a trainer I enjoyed immensely; that work helped inspire this book.

Storytelling is a powerful teaching tool, and I first introduced the fictional middle school principal, Mr. Crandall, and Trey, a social studies teacher who eventually became one of his best mentors, in my second book, *The Active Teacher* (2010). Their story is continued and concluded in this volume.

Finally, and tragically, we are losing teachers faster in this country than is either desirable or necessary. Induction programs and well-trained and dedicated mentors can make a difference, as we shall see in the following pages.

Enjoy.

1

The Need for Heroes

In my workshops around the country, I ask educators to remember and give some thought to memorable teachers from their past who alternately pushed and pulled, expected and inspected, stood their ground when it came to quality student work, and accepted no excuses on the road to developing talent, skills, and young minds. Having instructed workshop participants—themselves often new or aspiring teachers—to describe their teacher heroes, I listen closely and never fail to note the passion with which they tell their stories. In their discussions, they will invariably tick off a list of characteristics, beliefs, and actions that placed these remembered and revered teachers in the top tier of educators. Listening to these workshop participants share, I am always reminded that they understand that teachers matter, and the best teachers matter most.

Schools can be new and expensive; they can boast the latest in technological advances; they can be beautifully landscaped, ecologically sound, and replete with resources and materials—yet, as Whitaker (2004) reminds us, "without great teachers, the school lacks the keystone of greatness" (p. 9). And, good teachers *do* make a difference for students. In an analysis of studies in several states and districts, Haycock (1998) reaffirms what has always made sense to me: Effective teachers get more out of students than less effective teachers, and the gap widens with low achievers. In Tennessee, in 1996, research done by Sanders and Rivers (Haycock, 1998) showed that the most effective teachers showed student-improvement gains of 39 percentage points more than the least effective teachers when working with low-achieving students (Haycock, p. 3). In looking at the research on teacher effectiveness, Haycock also concluded that while content knowledge is critical, especially at the secondary level, it is most effective when combined with teaching skills (p. 6). A good teacher induction program ought to combine professional development focused on improvement of teaching skills with college courses or other training geared toward improving content knowledge.

In almost four decades in education, I have come to the conclusion that there are (at least) nine qualities shared by highly effective teachers. Having observed hundreds of classrooms over the past 16 years, these qualities seem to be present in classrooms where achievement and morale are high, where time and energy are not wasted, and where students respect their teachers and enjoy coming to school. In less-effective classrooms, these qualities are often lacking; and in those cases, the body language of students—and often teachers—runs the gamut from indifference to outright hostility. Referencing great teachers and highlighting what makes them powerful role models is useful in demonstrating for new—or veteran—teachers that to which they can aspire.

In the next few pages, I'll explore these nine qualities. At the same time, I'll begin to look at new teacher induction and mentoring in the context of these qualities by offering suggestions to administrators and mentors alike. I certainly don't claim this list is in any way complete, but I do believe that exceptional teachers

1. Avoid the blame game and instead focus on affecting learning;

2. Anticipate what *might* happen, plan ahead, and work at perfecting procedures individually and collectively when possible;

3. Learn to listen, build quality relationships, and enjoy coming to school every day;

4. Understand that the students need to do 80% of the work done in the classroom;

5. Function as process facilitators rather than purveyors of information;

6. Work on improving student performance, letting the tests take care of themselves;

7. Provide a consistently calm and steady keel on which students can rely;

8. Commit to a personal and professional continuous-improvement process; and

9. Enlist humor as a motivator and encourage much laughter in the classroom.

Avoid the blame game and instead focus on affecting learning

I can remember entering many a faculty lounge in my earliest years as a teacher, and as much as possible, I avoided long sojourns there because of the negative commentary that (along with the smoke) seemed to permeate the atmosphere. On occasion, I fell prey to playing that game—blaming the parents, the students, the curriculum, the textbooks, the administration, and (always) the lack of time. The irony of spending my free time *complaining that there was not enough time* escaped me in those early days in the profession.

Jenkins (2003), says that blaming fixes nothing, allows those in charge to escape responsibility (as everyone tries to fix blame on someone or something else), and perhaps worst of all, it "stops the search for underlying causes," meaning that what needs fixed remains broken, and badly needed progress is either slowed or stopped in its tracks (p. xxvi). In a collaborative and risk-free school culture, where teacher leaders are free—and indeed encouraged—to pursue practical solutions, no one has time for playing the blame game because they are too busy brainstorming ideas, solving problems, and improving instruction. Those school environments that are essentially isolationist and where a top-down management style is the rule, teachers may be left to solve their own problems (without the capacity to do that effectively) or simply ignore them—and play the blame game day after day.

Mr. Crandall, the fictitious principal whom we met in the Prologue, long ago abandoned isolationism and a top-down management style for one of collaboration, experimentation, and innovation. Trey, along with others who served as mentors, knew they could experiment and take risks based on a set of core principles in operation all year long. The fear that can permeate an autocratic schoolhouse environment and impede growth was markedly absent in that middle school. Shellie and the other new teachers were fortunate to be part of a collegial staff that included support personnel like teacher assistants, office staff, and custodians. It was the custodial staff in Shellie's school that readily agreed to prepare her classroom first, along with those of the other new teachers, so that they could use July and early August to get everything arranged. Mr. Crandall knew that teachers who could get a good deal of the logistical preparation out of the way early on were much more likely to enter the school year in a positive frame of mind.

Teachers are much more likely to complain on a regular basis if the overall climate of the schoolhouse is negative and if regular support is lacking. New teachers entering this environment may begin to identify with the "negaholics" in the building, especially if October and November bring a deterioration of discipline in the new teacher's classroom. Lacking a strong and effective support system, new teachers may try to find someone to blame for their predicament, or they may simply get so discouraged they leave the profession early.

Administrators would do well to make certain that mentors are chosen from among the ranks of positive teachers; mentors should not be chosen simply because they know the subject matter or because they have been in the school a long time and therefore know all the ins and outs of the building and culture. Administrators should also create an atmosphere where positive behavior is encouraged *and modeled at the top.* The object here is to swell the ranks of those who refuse to blame others and instead take responsibility for their own actions. One way to decrease the number of those who play the blame game is to spend a good deal of time with the faculty searching for root causes of problems and then solving those problems as part of a regular and predictable continuous-improvement process.

Anticipate what **might** *happen, plan ahead, and work at perfecting procedures individually and collectively when possible*

Great teachers do not waste time, nor do they react in an unpredictable fashion to what happens in the classroom. The best teachers I have observed over the years are those who take the first week of school to turn procedures into routines. Many superb teachers I know refuse to hand out textbooks or other subject-area materials until students practice over and over having structured and purposeful conversations with everyone in the class. Those teachers practice bringing students back to them with a visual signal until the kids have it down to a few seconds. In those classrooms, procedures for setting up, cleaning up, and lining up are practiced until they become routine. Before anything is said about history, reading, math, or science, students are primed and ready to function as members of an efficient and productive classroom culture in which they learn they can share and contribute constructively in an emotionally safe environment. This kind of procedural consistency can often be a powerful part of the total collective—and collaborative—school environment.

In 2008, I visited an outstanding school, Sanders Corner Elementary, located in Loudoun County, Virginia. While walking through the hallways with Principal Kathy Hwang, I observed groups of students walking quickly, quietly, and safely from one room to another. This procedure of moving in an orderly fashion was in evidence no matter where we traveled in the school for over thirty minutes.

This did not just happen, and it did not come about as a result of a memo or edict. Sanders Corner is a school with an active and effective leadership team dedicated to continuous improvement. Hwang related that in a brainstorming session concerning what could be improved, the teachers suggested the hallways were consistently noisy—something that had a negative effect on classes all over the building. Hwang did not *prescribe* anything by way of a cure; she simply asked the teachers to consider what they thought might be done about it. She realized that by reflecting on both the problem and possible solutions, her staff was fully capable of solving the problem on their own.

They came up with the idea of instituting a schoolwide procedure for making the hallways quiet, something that involved practicing walking quietly in the hallways for many days. On occasion, teachers would hear talking in the ranks, and they would simply turn around, stop the students with a hand signal, and point back toward the room. The students would turn around and go back, starting over again—this time quietly. Teachers did not shout, complain, or scold. They simply took the students back to the room, doing it all over again until they got it right. What I observed was the result of many weeks of work as part of an overall commitment to respectful behavior in the school.

Great teachers—and *all* the teachers at Sanders Corner Elementary—understand that positive and predictable results come from planning and thinking about what *could* go wrong; considering in advance what *might* happen; and in the case of this faculty, working together to find a common solution to what they agreed was a considerable—and common—problem. This requires frontloading, and while some teachers may come to this kind of proactive planning instinctively, others can come to it in their turn when collaboration and innovation are the norm in the schoolhouse. Sanders Corner principal, Kathy Hwang, and her entire staff work together in an atmosphere where the blame game is not acceptable and collaboration is the norm.

New teachers need to understand that the process horse comes before the content cart, and administrators and mentors can work with protégés to frontload their own classroom system with solid procedures, rules, and beliefs that can jump start a great year. This is why Trey and Mr. Crandall began to work with Shellie immediately; Trey met with her soon after she signed her contract, and the summer became far less apprehensive for Shellie and the other three new teachers because administrators, teammates, and her mentor, Trey, took it upon themselves to make her feel at home and anticipate questions and potential problems well in advance of the first week of school for students. Trey was a fantastic teacher, and he understood the value of frontloading the process with proper planning, but it was the *system* at the school that best served Shellie. Trey could have retired at any time, but the *system* at that school would take over and assist Shellie in her first years in the profession.

Once again, while great teachers may come to this frontloading process naturally, every teacher can work toward being proactive, using the summer to think about what *might* happen and what *might* arise over the course of the school year. Mentors can help new teachers reflect on the coming year as a way of surfacing issues that can be part of the planning process necessary to a smooth-functioning classroom.

Learn to listen, build quality relationships, and enjoy coming to school every day

Along the road in my professional journey, I had occasion to serve as a salesman and sales manager for a school yearbook printing company. On one rather memorable (in the way painful experiences can be memorable) occasion, I had spent the better part of 40 minutes presenting the highlights of our program to a school principal and his yearbook adviser. I had prepared what I perceived was a superb presentation that would captivate and engage them, and ultimately result in my getting the contract for the following year. I had spent a good deal of time the night before constructing a great plan that could not help but succeed, and I let it rip for those 40 minutes. When I was done I was exhausted, but confident I had made my case.

While I put away my displays and sample books, the principal and yearbook adviser went to his office to talk it over, and in a few minutes the adviser came back, thanked me for my presentation, and said the principal would like to see me. I walked confidently down the hall, and his secretary took me in to meet with him, shutting the door on her way out. He began by saying, "You did *not* get the contract for next year, but I like you, so I'm going to tell you why and give you some advice." He went on to say that in those 40 minutes all I did was talk. I did not try to get to know him or his yearbook adviser. I did not even ask *what they wanted* in a yearbook program. I had made no attempt to build any kind of relationship. Finally, there were a great many things in what I had offered that they could not afford and/or did not want, but I had not taken the time to find out what they *did* want or need. In short, I simply did not listen. I did not ask questions. I made no attempt at building a relationship. *I just talked for 40 minutes.*

I learned a valuable lesson from that experience relatively early in my sales career, and the lesson carried over to my reentry into teaching a few years later: Even the best-designed lesson plan can't overcome the absence of relationship building, and this applies in teaching as it applies in sales. To put this in very practical terms, no one will buy what you're selling *until they buy you.* Salespeople and teachers who ignore this basic principle will see otherwise beautifully constructed plans fail for a lack of planning in the all-important building of meaningful relationships. Part of putting the process horse before the content cart involves foundational relationship building that ensures students are in the right frame of mind for the content they know will follow. Great teachers learn to do far more listening than talking.

Bondy and Ross (2008) affirm that, especially when it comes to high-poverty schools, well-designed lesson plans are not enough if students are not engaged (p. 54). Rather than waiting and hoping relationships magically develop in the classroom, great teachers build relationships deliberately and work to get to know students on a daily basis and in many seemingly small, but effective, ways: "A smile, a hand on the shoulder, the use of a student's name, or a question that shows you remember something the student has mentioned—these small gestures do much to develop relationships" (Bondy & Ross, 2008, pp. 55–56).

The (relatively few) great teachers and professors from my past made the time to get to know me, and they paid attention to my talents and to what I enjoyed doing. These teachers stand out in my mind because they cared about me and demonstrated that with what they said and did; their actions supported their words. Mentors need to spend time with their protégés reflecting on the qualities of their own great teachers. It may be that these outstanding educators inspired the protégé to become a teacher in the first place. It is not difficult to imagine that what new teachers see in their heroes is that to which they aspire. Uncovering those natural aspirations as part of a reflective process may well serve as a good starting point for mentors who desire to develop their own personal and professional relationship with the protégé looking to them for support. Mentors need to be as proactive in developing relationships with new teachers as new teachers are in developing relationships with the students in their care.

Over the years, I have seen enough negative teacher attitudes to convince me that negativity is as destructive as it is contagious. There are people who have the ability to drain a meeting or classroom of every positive aspect; I call them the negaholics. They drag themselves to school every day and admittedly (and vocally) wish they were somewhere else. The antidote to this malady is a schoolhouse climate that is pervasively and consistently positive; it is an environment that does not give in to the negaholics and eventually either changes them, neutralizes them, or chases them away.

New teachers need mentors who love coming to school every day; they need mentors who will help them learn to navigate *on their own* the somewhat rocky shoals of even the most positive school climate. Bluestein (2008) encourages teachers to develop a "self-caring behavior" that helps us "avoid or minimize our exposure to negative people, information, or influences" (p. 259). A new teacher who finds he or she has no way to deflect, deal with, or ignore these negative influences is in for a long school year and may enjoy coming to school less each day. Mentors can help novice teachers come up with a plan to stay positive (and effective) in the face of those who have become both negative (and ineffective) over the years.

Understand that the students need to do 80% of the work done in the classroom

No coach ever lectured his or her way to the big game on Friday night, and no player ever joined the basketball team to watch the coach . . . well . . . *coach.* The only way kids on a team are going to improve is to be part of an effective feedback loop. The coach models; the players *do;* the coach provides feedback; the players incorporate the feedback into a new level of doing; the coach provides more feedback—and both the individual players and the team improve as the learning curve moves inexorably in an upward direction. One of the best teachers I know uses this same feedback cycle with her fifth graders. She models, and then they *do;* she provides feedback, and they incorporate the feedback into a new level of doing. The beat goes on, the grades go up, and the kids . . . well . . . they love being in that classroom, and they are totally engaged.

My major in college was history, and my first teaching position was eighth-grade United States history. I was determined to display for those students the depth and breadth of my knowledge, not realizing that my job should have been to develop the depth and breadth of *their* thinking and knowledge. I lectured, showed educational videos and filmstrips, administered countless quizzes and tests, and gave them the benefit of my understanding of the subject area. I entertained, I explained, I elucidated, I assigned—in short, I did most of the work. They sat, they listened, they read out loud, they took notes, they smiled—and they went to a better place in their minds while I rattled on, oblivious to their lack of engagement.

In the faculty lounge the teachers, most of whom were doing most of the work, complained about the work ethic (or lack thereof) on the part of the students. It never occurred to us that we did not give them much to do; we did not give them a chance to explain, elucidate, entertain, infer, compare, contrast, give examples, or otherwise become involved in their own learning. In short, students learn more by being engaged in something than they do by simply watching teachers work. The great teachers understand this and engage students at every turn.

One of my favorite teachers was a sixth-grade language arts teacher who clearly understood that if we were to improve our writing skills we had to write. We wrote frequently, and we received mountains of feedback. We learned punctuation in the context of the sentences, paragraphs, essays, and poems we wrote. We used up tons of tablets and # 2 pencils—and we learned through doing. There were blackboards on three walls, and we were constantly on our feet practicing our writing skills while she provided individual feedback and encouragement. Each of us moved more or less quickly along the continuous-improvement highway, but in my case I discovered a love for words and a passion for the ways in which they wielded power in combination with one another. She modeled; then, she let us do what we needed to do in order to get better while providing practical and immediate feedback.

Students who are engaged in a task need feedback that is, according to Marzano, Pickering, and Pollock (2001), corrective in nature, that is, feedback that "provides students with an explanation of what they are doing that is correct and what they are doing that is not correct" (p. 96). It is by doing, getting feedback, redoing, getting feedback, and redoing that students make progress along their own continuous-improvement pathways. Mentors would do well to have their protégés reflect on the efficacy of student engagement with meaningful work as opposed to the behavioral implications of having students disengaged (and disinterested?) in the classroom.

Function as process facilitators
rather than purveyors of information

Teachers in the industrial age were often one among a very few sources of information. The print resources of the school and local libraries, a personal set of encyclopedias (often woefully out of date), a textbook, and the classroom teacher provided the information base for students. One click of a computer mouse today can open the electronic doorways to a seemingly limitless amount of information on any subject imaginable. *Wikipedia*, the online encyclopedia, is constantly and instantly updated, and it is free. Teachers today have shifted from being one among a very few sources of *information* to helping students sort through and *make sense* of the mountainous amount of information to which they have immediate access at all hours of the day or night.

Today's teachers need to be process facilitators, according to Allen (2010), giving students strategies for "coping with large amounts of information," and helping them uncover and learn "key ideas" on the road to developing ways to do this on their own throughout the course of their lives (p. 94). In this era of information overload, helping students deal with this involves not only helping them locate key ideas, but separating opinions from facts, making critical decisions, solving problems, and finding their way in a global economy. Doing all this requires critical thinking skills that great teachers of any era instill and develop in their students; skills that will help them survive and thrive in today's world.

One obstacle to dealing with this information-rich age as a teacher is that the teaching methods of the industrial age (lecture, videos, filmstrips, worksheets) have survived the transition because tradition is a powerful force. New teachers who were lectured to in high school and college may adopt this as their main delivery method with students used to rapid transitions on television and in video games. Images on TV change every few seconds, and students, according to Allen (2010), "developed shorter attention spans but increased their abilities to multitask and rapidly shift topics" (pp. 29–30). Today's highly effective teachers have adapted their delivery methods to this new reality, and mentors need to reflect with novice teachers on the efficacy of shifting tasks and activities frequently, perhaps every few minutes. Short periods of lecture can be followed by student-to-student conversations on the topic, and short video clips followed by a discussion can replace the showing of entire 30-minute segments. Worksheets can be replaced by a visual display on the screen, with students in trios or quartets discussing that information on their feet. Mentors can arrange for protégés to observe classrooms in which teaching and learning have come together in the capable hands of teachers who have adapted to the new reality.

Work on improving student performance,
letting the tests take care of themselves

We have become a nation of testers, and we as educators too often succumb to what Bluestein (2008) calls the "obsession for testing" and "lust for high scores" that has become pervasive in the United States (p. 269). Fear of not reaching a benchmark on state testing drives schools and teachers to teach to the test and sometimes reduce physical activity in favor of seat time. Teachers who fear falling behind in the race to "cover the curriculum" choose pacing over depth and form over substance. That race to the state-testing finish line may exhaust teachers and students alike, and it can frustrate everyone in the process.

The very best teachers I have seen over the years concentrate on steady improvement over time, with feedback and formative assessments providing students with critical information about what they are doing correctly and incorrectly along the way. These teachers do not worry about the state tests. They understand that students who enjoy coming to school every day and are not afraid to take risks in a safe classroom environment will take care of the end-of-year or end-of-course tests. The great teachers understand it is the kids that need to do most of the work while they facilitate process and provide feedback in the name of continuous improvement. In the other two volumes in this series, *The Active Classroom* (2008) and *The Active Teacher* (2010), I have mentioned Cindy Rickert, a superb fifth-grade teacher. Her students actually look forward to the tests at the end of the year, and they can't wait to see the results—no wonder, because for three years in a row all her students passed the state writing test . . . and hers is the inclusion team!

A sports team that is well led in practice by a coach who understands the continuous-improvement process will win its share of games—without worrying overmuch about the games or their results. Games are won in practice, and tests are passed because great teachers know how to engage and involve students in their own learning . . . and ably facilitate that process over time. Once again, mentors need to provide opportunities for their protégés to see teachers who do this well inside and outside their own schools or districts. Find those teachers, and arrange for protégés to spend a day observing how those powerful and effective teachers do what they do.

Provide a consistently calm and steady keel on which students can rely

Every teacher in the country ought to have these two phrases of Dr. Fred Jones (2007) engraved above the classroom door, painted on each floor tile, and inserted at the bottom of every lesson plan:

> ## CALM IS STRENGTH.
> ## UPSET IS WEAKNESS.

Great teachers understand that staying calm in the face of adversity is a definite advantage for a teacher. Jones (2007) puts it this way, "You will never be able to control a classroom until you are first *in control of yourself*" (p. 180). Teacher mentors need to spend time on this with novice teachers, once again reflecting on classroom situations where teachers were either in or out of control as a matter of course.

I had occasion once to visit a classroom where the teacher closed the classroom door and verbally berated the students with considerable force, blaming them for something even I could see was the teacher's fault and not theirs. The rules posted in the classroom called for mutual respect, something that appeared to be lacking, as evidenced by this temper tantrum on the part of the teacher. In such an atmosphere, nothing much happens by way of improvement or learning. I have also been in classrooms where a pervasive calm and safe climate served as the perfect medium for progress. Taking risks or surfacing curiosity was possible in those classrooms in a way that would have been impossible in that first—and completely dysfunctional—classroom.

Schools that have professional libraries (usually within the school library) should stock them with books that deal with creating school and classroom environments conducive to learning, safe for the risk takers, and encouraging to the merely curious among students and faculty alike. The months prior to the start of the school year are perfect for conversation and reflection among all the mentors and protégés, and a well-appointed professional-development library might be a great place to meet and begin the relationship-building process. Again, mentors and administrators can make arrangements for new teachers to see cool, calm, and effective teachers in action.

Commit to a personal and professional continuous-improvement process

Teachers are in the continuous-improvement business. The object is to help Eddie do something today he could not do yesterday, and to assist Eddie and his classmates in their own steady and relentless progress along many fronts. Working with students to set and achieve goals constitutes an important part of their continuous-improvement journey, and teachers need to be relentless in that pursuit of excellence. Students and parents, on the other hand, have every right to expect that teachers be fully committed to their own continuous-improvement efforts.

In our determination to get well when we are ill or stay well when we are healthy again, we enlist the support of medical professionals whom we trust to be current with the latest in medical knowledge and skills. We want our doctors to know everything there is to know about the human body, and we rely on them to avail themselves of every bit of professional development at their disposal. By the same token, students and parents have every right to expect that the teachers in whom they place the education of their children know as much as possible about how the brain operates as it pertains to learning. Since what science is discovering about how the brain functions grows at an ever-increasing rate, teachers and the administrators who support them need to put in place professional-development programs that will ultimately facilitate the intellectual growth and educational progress of students and teachers alike.

Mentors need to arrange for protégés to observe highly effective and successful teachers inside and outside their own buildings (and districts). New teachers need to be part of a collective effort at continuous improvement within the schoolhouse. Faculty meetings can move from being information dumps to becoming opportunities to work on instructionally related issues. Book clubs can help teachers stay abreast of the latest research in the field, and groups of teachers can look at assessment data with an eye toward improving instruction and closing gaps. New teachers who are part of a professional learning community early on will benefit by developing good habits early in their careers. For these less-experienced teachers, Hord and Sommers (2008) maintain, "the connectedness that grows out of studying, learning, and finding new ways to be effective will provide meaning for themselves personally and make a difference professionally" (p. 150).

In observing highly effective teachers in their classrooms, I have noticed that they are constantly trying new strategies and adjusting old ones. One teacher regularly elicits the feedback of students after introducing something new in order to get their perspectives. Keeping what works, discarding what doesn't, and introducing new ideas into the mix can ensure that teachers and students consistently move forward in their own continuous-improvement model. While the best teachers seem to do this instinctively, helping novice teachers adopt a model for continuous improvement is something mentors and building administrators can and should do. A teacher who gets in the improvement habit early is going to need much less help or intervention later on in his career.

Enlist humor as a motivator and encourage much laughter in the classroom

My favorite college professor had an incredible sense of humor, and his lectures were replete with funny stories and asides that made us laugh . . . and encouraged us to listen lest we miss anything. A junior high school history teacher told terrible jokes. He knew they were terrible; we knew they were terrible; *he* knew that *we* knew they were terrible . . . and that was rather the point. We laughed—and groaned loudly as I recall—at each joke and somehow looked forward to the next one. Many teachers I have observed have demonstrated a marvelous ability to use self-deprecating humor that displayed a heaping helping of self-confidence.

I have seen some pretty tense classroom situations defused by laughter, and I have seen some classrooms where laughter is discouraged because it "takes away from the business at hand." McCutcheon and Lindsey (2006) says that being humorous is not about telling jokes one after the other but is "simply a matter of creating an environment in which students are given permission to chuckle or chortle or even cackle" (p. 236). It turns out that chuckling, chortling, and cackling are healthy as well. According to Smith (2005), laughter has beneficial effects on blood pressure, depression, and cognition (p. 162). Smith says that "people are better able to deal with cognitive challenge when they approach the challenge through shared laughter with others" (p. 162). Laughter is beneficial, then, on many levels, and mentors should work with protégés to encourage its use.

Administrators, official teacher mentors, and those who are

Mentor/Protégé Focus

No matter when teachers are hired, during the spring, summer, or just prior to the beginning of the new school year, teacher mentors need to make certain their protégés are provided with opportunities to observe veteran teachers who exemplify great teaching.

enlisted in the new-teacher induction process at the school level would do well to reflect on these (and other) qualities shared by highly effective teachers. There is one other thing teachers who embrace these nine qualities have in common—they get results in the way of performance and student satisfaction. New teachers should visit the classrooms of those teachers (anywhere they can be found) who demonstrate the best qualities and get the best results. In every school district there are teachers who have built into their classroom instruction and management system a continuous-improvement model capable of facilitating progress every year. Once the leadership team of a building identifies these outstanding teachers, the next step is to get new teachers (all teachers in fact) into those classrooms.

Final Thoughts

Any single person or team in charge of a districtwide or schoolwide new-teacher induction program should identify those teachers, principles, and qualities that together set the qualitative standard to which new teachers or even veterans new to the district or individual school should aspire. The qualities successfully internalized by highly effective teachers are well worth emulating. In Chapter 2, we'll explore what a powerful new-teacher induction program might look like before moving into the role of the teacher mentor in Chapter 3.

2

The Need for Speed

S hellie, the new teacher we met in the Prologue, was fortunate to land in a school where the administration and faculty had in place a fully developed support system—not just for new teachers but for everyone on staff. Shellie's college roommate was not so fortunate, and her attempts to stand virtually alone as the rains came and the winds blew were ultimately unsuccessful. Having received four years of preparation to become a teacher, Shellie's friend found herself outside the profession after one school year, taking a job as a receptionist. Shellie, on the other hand, did not have to weather the storms alone, and she signed a contract in May to continue as a member of the faculty for a second year.

If, as we saw earlier, we are losing one-third of our new teachers by their third year in the profession, and by as much as 50% within five years (Grissmer & Kirby, 1997), we need to take a close look at *why* this is happening, with an eye toward stemming the flow. It is true that some people may not be cut out for teaching; and for some, no matter how much support is available, they—and their students— would be better off if they left for jobs where their talents allowed them to be more effective. There are also teachers who will succeed despite difficulties and obstacles because they are naturally more resilient and therefore capable of "assessing adverse situations, recognizing options for coping, and arriving at appropriate solutions" (Bobek, 2001, p. 202). The vast majority of new teachers will always need considerable support from colleagues, school administration, and district-level instructional specialists and coaches.

As with any profession where those who enter look forward to a long and satisfying career, the early years for teachers are critical. Habits, good or bad, will be established during this formative period, and teachers who are simply left to react to events as they unfold will find themselves at the mercy of the tide's ebb and flow. Mistakes are made during those first weeks, months, and years; without the valuable perspectives and feedback of other professionals, teachers are left to fend for themselves—often to the detriment of their own personal development and the educational progress of the students in their care. Simply handing new teachers the keys to their rooms without providing them with the keys to continuous improvement is counterproductive. We cannot assume novice teachers know all they need to know about facilitating the continuous-improvement journey of 30 fifth graders or over 100 freshmen. Dealing with problems day after day leads many teachers to the conclusion that the grass may be greener somewhere outside their classrooms.

Some statistics: According to Ingersoll and Smith (2004), almost 30% of new teachers change schools or leave teaching at the end of the first year in the classroom. Additionally, from the beginning of the 1990s to the year 2000, the number of teachers reporting they had been part of an induction program rose from less than 50% to almost 80% (Ingersoll & Smith, 2004, p. 706). This increase is to a great extent a recognition of the need to retain teachers, but the question remains as to how extensive and how effective those programs are. Ingersoll and Smith (2004) found that the more successful induction programs had multiple components, such as mentors in the same subject area and collaboration with colleagues; and, they state that "teachers participating in combinations or packages of mentoring and group induction activities were less likely to migrate to other schools or to leave teaching at the end of their first year" (p. 706).

Not providing support at least at the school level is expensive, not only for the district that has to replace a teacher who left in frustration, but for the students who did not receive the kind of education they deserve—even from a new teacher. Bransford, Darling-Hammond, and LePage (2005) state that "these students, like all others, are entitled to sound instruction and cannot afford to lose a year of schooling to a teacher who is ineffective or learning by trial and error on the job" (p. 3). Add to the reasons to provide induction programs in all schools and districts the fact that students are the ultimate beneficiaries of such support mechanisms.

The first component of a successful schoolwide induction program would seem to be a collaborative atmosphere where all teachers, not just those new to the profession, have traded isolationism for collaboration and mutual support. The collaborative climate is one where learning on the part of teachers is always in fashion, and continuous improvement is not just a

> ## Mentor/Protégé Focus
>
> *Teachers are full of anticipation when they are hired, and they may also be apprehensive in this totally new professional situation and physical setting. At the first opportunity, mentors need to activate the school's support system (administrators and teacher leaders, office staff, custodians, specialists, and other teachers) with an eye toward making the new teacher decide she made the right choice in accepting this job.*

buzzword. Shellie, the new teacher from the Prologue, found herself in just such an environment. It began as soon as she was hired, and Trey, her mentor, facilitated her involvement in every facet of the professional-development side of school life. Trey arranged for Shellie to observe two excellent teachers in May, as soon as she was hired. Trey and the principal, Mr. Crandall, made sure that Shellie had already met many of the teachers before everyone reported back in August. She had met with her own Cardinal team twice during the summer, and her room was ready early, something made possible by having the custodial staff place all four new teachers at the top of the priority scale when it came to classroom preparation. In short, Shellie had every reason to appreciate her support system before school even started in late August.

Humans may be essentially social beings, but isolationist tendencies are predominant in too many schools. At Shellie's school, Mr. Crandall spent years breaking down barriers to create a sense of community and professional interdependency that served the needs of students as well as veteran and novice teachers alike. The connections with Shellie were made early and often, so that her first year was not one of isolation; indeed, it was filled with frequent and meaningful collaboration with colleagues, administrators, and staff. Westheimer (2008), says that "teachers, as much as students, require these attachments in order to live out satisfying professional lives in schools and create conditions of community for students" (p. 766). Teachers who are themselves part of a dynamic community of learning make it far easier for new teachers to create collaborative classrooms. The modeling is going on all around them, as became apparent to Shellie from the first time she met with Trey and others in her new school.

Before novice teachers can become competent at what they do, what they need to do must be made clear to them by administrators and teacher leaders. Too many teachers come into the classroom and, without any guidance or clear understanding of what truly effective teaching looks like, simply fall back on what may have become familiar in high school and college: lecture, videos, worksheets, and summative quizzes and tests in a format (multiple choice or true/false) that is easy to grade. Lacking a structured support system or a mentor who understands what effective instruction looks like, new teachers are likely to soldier on, reacting (often badly) to situations that arise for which they have no clue as to what to do. Without guidance or direction, new teachers will fall back on what they know.

In schools where collaboration, professional development, and an effective continuous-improvement model are already in place, teachers can, as Bransford et al. (2005) conclude, "come to know students and families well; work with other teachers to provide a coherent, well-grounded curriculum; evaluate and guide student progress using information-rich assessments; and use texts and materials that support thoughtful learning" (p. 4). Shellie and the other three new teachers at her school were welcomed into a fully functioning community dedicated to progress on the part of teachers and students alike. Her roommate, as Shellie subsequently discovered, spent a frustrating year in a school whose professional growth model seemed to be "Hang in there!" She didn't.

In developing a schoolwide induction program, administrators and teacher leaders involved in its creation need to think about just who is going into teaching today. Some incoming teachers are recent college graduates in their early 20's; there will be those who raised a family, went back to school, and are coming into the classroom in middle age. Still others may have chosen one of the alternative preparation programs springing up all over the country. These new teachers may come with 20 or 30 years in another profession, with life experience but less time to prepare for the new career they are embracing. There are many who spent years as teacher assistants while working their way through a traditional college program. Because the people coming into teaching today have such diverse backgrounds, this calls for flexibility in any support structure that is developed.

Schools would do well, then, to develop an induction program capable of supporting new teachers of every stripe, including teachers new to the school but not new to teaching. Careful thought should be given to the relative needs of career switchers and those fresh out of college. Even though some aspects of the developing program may be quite different, there will be some core consistencies that are nonnegotiable. For example, in the area of instruction, the entire school can be dedicated to students as active learners rather than passive observers. The use of engagement techniques, formative assessments that provide lots of feedback, and a reliance on the visual, auditory, and kinesthetic predicates can be modeled in classrooms as well as in professional development for teachers. If the school has a set of beliefs that serve as a foundation for all learning in the building, then this needs to be communicated effectively to every teacher (new or new to the schoolhouse) from the day of the original interview.

Becoming a community of learners also means becoming a community of *leaders*. There was never any doubt in the mind of Mr. Crandall that Trey would become a teacher leader, and building leadership capacity was always job one in Mr. Crandall's dynamic and collaborative management style. He worked each year to build a system that would outlive him. The last thing he wanted was to retire down the road, taking with him in his briefcase all the answers, solutions, and problem-solving tools—leaving his school functionally bankrupt and unable to make progress until another principal came along who had the answers, solutions, and problem-solving tools in his or her briefcase. In his dozen years as the school's principal, Mr. Crandall had created a continuous-improvement model that would function effectively without him.

Mr. Crandall had previously served as a teacher in a school with a my-way-or-the-highway mentality on the part of the building administrators. It was during those years that he began to explore Linda Lambert's work on building leadership capacity in schools. He vowed that if he ever became a principal, he would not follow the example of his own administrators' tendencies toward what Lambert (2003) described as autocratic leadership, a top-down information flow, the absence of a shared vision, and paternal/maternal relationships in the schoolhouse (p. 5). For his own part, Mr. Crandall observed the adverse effects of a school that played the blame game and refused to look in the collective mirror for root causes of low morale and poor student performance. He remained positive and worked to get his administrative degree at a local university. He spent three years as an assistant principal before moving to the middle school and his new position as principal.

In his first year at the new school, Mr. Crandall had begun to shift his new school community to what Lambert (2003) describes as a Quadrant 4 School, one in which a strong and clearly defined set of values and expectations formed the foundation for a collaborative, innovative, inquiry-based, and totally reflective environment (p. 5). Mr. Crandall began to work with parents, faculty, staff, and students to create a model of continuous improvement where stakeholders were valued and teachers and students were not afraid to take risks in the name of progress. Trey, who had originally been mentored by Mr. Crandall's own teacher mentor, Mrs. Slattery, was now on the way to becoming an assistant principal. Mentoring was not, as it is in many schools, the sum total of the induction program that had been crafted and improved over Mr. Crandall's tenure as principal; it was one critical component of a total system that supported new teachers for three years and in a very real way supported everyone in the building.

Teacher induction programs may differ in many ways, but if they are to be ultimately effective they must be built to outlast the tenure of the current administration. The whole idea of supporting teachers from every possible angle and in every possible way must be the guiding principle of a self-sustaining system so deeply ingrained in the fabric of the school community that no stakeholder could imagine life without it. If the leadership capacity of the building is limited to the official administrative level, and if no one else has a stake or a role in the survival of an induction program, it will not long survive. A program that develops with the active involvement of the stakeholders and is proved to be effective over time is far more likely to remain as a vibrant and extremely useful component in the school community's continuous-improvement process.

Just as teacher mentoring is one component of a school's overall induction program, the induction program cannot be run independently of the regular school environment. A culture that is negative and generally oppressive is not going to support a vibrant and effective induction program. Whatever is done for new teachers is most likely going to reflect what is done for all teachers, and all stakeholders ought to be invested in a school environment that will nurture and sustain a system dedicated to simultaneously developing new teachers and serving students in the process. Below are a few essential components administrators can begin to put in place in order to create a culture capable of assisting in the growth of a successful new-teacher induction program.

Create a School Climate Conducive to Risk Taking

In order to improve instructionally, teachers often have to experiment, innovate, and change how they do what they do. This may involve students moving and talking with each other as they process new information. One teacher told me she was informed by an administrator that she should keep her students seated and quiet, lest they disturb anyone in the hallway or in other classrooms. The hallway was like most other hallways, in that with the door closed and with cement blocks between the classrooms, having the kids stand and share information, explain concepts to each other, or otherwise interact on their feet would not have bothered anyone—and it would have gone a long way toward developing communication and processing skills needed by her students.

In an era when students of any age have a bias for action, staying seated for 30, 40, or 50 minutes is painful at best, and it causes kids to find ways to get up and move anyway, actions that can lead to confrontation and a desire on the part of the kids to want to leave the room and not return. In observing hundreds of classrooms over the years, I can say that the happiest classrooms I have seen are those in which teachers regularly get students up, moving, sharing, laughing, and otherwise interacting as part of the daily routine. In classrooms where students are seated and quiet for long periods of time, their role is a passive one, and their body language betrays their disinterest and boredom. For teachers, shifting from a passive classroom to an active one involves risk but carries with it the potential for success.

Teachers must feel that they can experiment and innovate in an attempt to improve instruction—and innovations are increasingly important for teachers still caught up in the industrial age as far as teaching methodology is concerned. In the 1950s and 1960s, students learned to listen and learn by rote, according to Allen (2010), something that suited them well to working in an economic world dominated by manufacturing and the assembly line:

> In stark contrast, Gen Y and Z graduates will primarily be employed as knowledge workers in services-based economies. In these economies, most repetitive functions are automated, and workers are valued for their ability to synthesize information, solve problems, think laterally, and be innovative. (p. 3)

This contextual economic shift requires that teachers be flexible in their methodology; students who are continually bombarded with information from every direction need to be able to think critically in order to make sense of it all. Shifting up the cognitive ladder from recalling to explaining (and giving examples), comparing and contrasting, inferring, defending, and evaluating will allow them to function effectively in a dynamic economy that takes competition out of the local and national arena and onto the global stage. Teachers must be able to take risks as they experiment and innovate in ways that will benefit their students.

District and building administrators need to take this into account, and new teachers need to be able to take risks on behalf of kids. New teachers need to work with mentors who not only understand this, but who will arrange for teachers to observe classrooms where risk taking, innovation, and teacher flexibility are interwoven into the continuous-improvement process. If a teacher who is trying something different in the interest of student progress is discouraged from doing so time and again, it may not be too long before he simply gives up and falls back into a familiar routine. Taking risks should be part of the entire school's culture, and when the risks pay off—or when they don't—the results can be shared with everyone on staff in order that they, too, may learn. New and interesting strategies can be tried by a great many teachers so that they can meet later and reflect on the results.

Mentor/Protégé Focus

Early in the relationship-building process, mentors should let protégés know that taking risks on behalf of kids is part of continuous improvement. Taking risks, getting feedback, and making adjustments are all essential to improving process, performance, and results.

Experimentation on behalf of kids should be encouraged by the administration as part of the overall professional-development program. A successful professional-development program will help new teachers and veterans alike, and as we will see in Chapter 3, it will make the lives of mentors a lot easier as they work to facilitate the professional growth of their protégés.

Replace Isolationist Tendencies With Collegiality and Collaboration

Teachers who work in isolation day after day see the world—and their curricula and students—through one set of glasses. I can report that this is exactly what I experienced my first year of teaching. I fell into a pattern in the classroom: lecture, asking questions of my "fan club" in every class, educational videos, review, quizzes, tests, and the ubiquitous worksheets. This was hardly powerful stuff, but it was what I knew. Left alone, looking at everything that happened and everything I did from this single perspective, led to little in the way of innovation. Early in my career, I did participate in "team teaching," but while this experience allowed for some interaction and sharing of ideas, it was not focused, and I still basically closed my classroom door and did my own thing day after day. My second team teaching experience, in the early 1990s, was much different, and our team was encouraged to take risks—which we did frequently—and this benefited not only the faculty on our seventh-grade team but our students as well.

It was through the eyes of a wonderful special education teacher on our inclusion team that I first saw the basic flaws in my instructional delivery system. I began to loosen up a bit; I lectured less and got the kids actively involved more frequently. One group of students wrote a play together in class, and the contextual richness of the process and the finished product improved their understanding—and their grades—in a unit on slavery. Working with special education students finally made me understand that the kinesthetic goes with the auditory and the visual to weave a wonderful and beautiful tapestry of learning. I learned to give the students many more choices as to assignments, and I finally understood that as teachers we can look through the lenses of our colleagues in order to learn, experiment, and innovate. Those two years on the inclusion team were the best two years of my teaching career, and I owe it to some wonderful teammates and the fact that they helped me discard my isolationist tendencies, built up over years of seeing everything from one perspective.

Principals can encourage collegiality and collaboration on the staff by modeling it when teachers get together for professional-development workshops (replacing faculty meetings that can so often be devoted to a series of speakers providing information that could easily be sent via e-mail) on school time. Administrators and teacher leaders can see to it that the school's professional-development library is well stocked with journals and books related to the art and science of teaching (in my opinion, a great use of PTA money), and that teachers are provided with time to form book groups that can— and should—share what they have learned with the faculty. Principals can also insist that teachers observe other classrooms, and that these observations are made with an eye toward looking for one or two specific things that the observer and the observed can talk about later on. Principals might also use money from the substitute teacher budget line to allow teachers to visit classrooms in other schools in the school district or in the region.

Everyone Is Responsible

In isolationist schools, there may be a perception that mentoring new teachers is in the hands of the teacher mentors alone, with everyone else continuing to do his or her thing, unaffected by the mentor-protégé program. Portner (2005a) calls this *"shortsighted and a prescription for failure"* (p. 76), and he uses the term *collaborative-doing* to describe a situation where "a wide variety of committed people" are actively involved in the induction process (p. 78). Specifically, this supporting cast is responsible for

1. Developing, monitoring, and adjusting their induction policies and procedures;

2. Interacting directly with new teachers to supplement the efforts of mentors; and

3. Supporting new teachers by providing them with time, facilities, and materials. (Portner, 2005a, p. 78)

New teachers to whom it is clear that the entire faculty and staff are committed to their development are far more likely to succeed than in situations where they are left pretty much on their own to sink or swim. Mentors who know this additional assistance for protégés is widely available in the building may well be appreciative of the fact that an effective induction system is operating in a powerful support role. Every professional in the schoolhouse should look at their active and positive involvement in assisting new teachers *as an investment in everyone's success*. Successful teachers have a positive and lasting effect on the school's ultimate progress. Figure 2.1 provides a look at how diverse members of the school community can actively assist new teachers.

Provide Ongoing Professional Development

Mentoring should not exist as the *sole* induction program of any school; mentoring should instead be one essential component of that overall support system. Powerful induction programs are much more than that and "are comprehensive, last several years, have clearly articulated goals, and provide a structured and nurturing system of professional development and support" (Wong, 2005, p. 43).

Figure 2.1

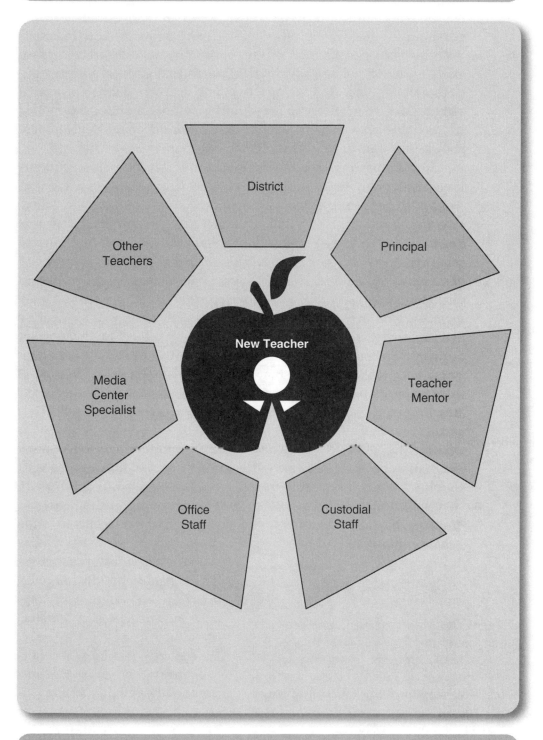

Additionally, according to Wong, "For a mentor to be effective, the mentor must be trained and then used in combination with the other components of the induction process" (p. 45). In professional learning communities the same professional-development structure that supports the induction program also supports the continuous-improvement goals of the school as a whole. This means that support for protégés does not cease at the end of one, two, or even three years. The formal mentor-protégé relationship may drop away, but the support provided by a viable and collaborative system of professional development should continue beyond that official time frame.

Continuous improvement is not an end; it is a process. Students benefit best by what Zmuda, Kuklis, and Kline (2004) call a *competent system* that shifts teachers from "individual autonomy to collective autonomy and collective accountability" (p. 1). Such a system begins with a "shared vision that articulates a coherent picture of what the school will look like when its core beliefs are put into practice" (Zmuda et al., 2004, p. 1). Most schools have many excellent teachers. Schools that embrace a systemic approach to improvement in all aspects also have excellent teachers; the difference is that in those schools there is a relentless and collective effort on the part of administrators and faculty members to improve the quality of learning from top to bottom. In that kind of system, the route to a powerful new-teacher induction program is a short one *for the simple reason that the professional-development framework for its support is already in place.*

New teachers, once they have been around for a few weeks, will begin to notice whether or not there is a strong commitment to continuous improvement in their building. If isolationism is rampant, they will notice that as well. Any mentoring program that tries to emphasize reflection and innovation in a school that seems to value *neither* is going to find the going rough. A school community whose professional-development system is completely in line with their shared vision will support new teachers and veterans alike.

Ask any group of teachers to identify their most precious commodity, and they will invariably tell you it is *time*. This being so, administrators can demonstrate that they, too,

---

Mentor/Protégé Focus

Mentors, using the school's professional development library or their own resources, should expose protégés to what works in classrooms by sharing articles from professional journals with them. If the mentor and protégé each read an article, for example, they can subsequently discuss key points with each other and reflect on application possibilities.

value time by turning faculty meetings that are often info dumps into valuable blocks of time where teachers and administrators can focus on instruction. Teachers who may not have the time to conduct research into what works in classrooms will be glad to know that there is a veritable cornucopia of research available to teachers and administrators concerning what works in classrooms. Beyond that, administrators can facilitate conversations about what works with teachers on their own faculty.

In faculty meetings or in smaller groups, teachers can look at performance data that can often reveal what is not otherwise visible, especially to novice teachers. Schmoker (1999) affirms that "data can convey the magnitude of a problem; they can arrest our attention, establish our priorities, and reveal progress that motivates and sustains us in our efforts" (p. 46). It is important that new teachers understand the role of data in a continuous-improvement model; it is critical that they see a faculty and administration completely caught up in collaborative efforts focused on instruction and results. It is one thing to read about this as part of an assignment in a teacher-preparation program; it is quite another to see it in action. New teachers need to be part of a school community that values professional development as a collaborative effort that will continue far beyond the official limits of a formal induction program.

Seek Feedback Constantly, Using It to Make Program Adjustments

In order to keep new teachers from leaving the profession, schools and districts must have induction programs that are continually evaluated and adjusted. The opinions of mentors, protégés, and everyone even remotely involved in the induction program should be solicited on a regular basis. A regular evaluation form can be sent out one or more times per year in order to determine how well the induction program is doing. The resultant feedback should be used to make everything from minor adjustments to major changes in the program. New teachers at the end of their first, second, and third years can be contacted in order to see if the level of support at each level is adequate or in need of revision. This can be done at the district or school level, but it needs to be done. No one is closer to the program than mentors and protégés, and they will appreciate an administration that invites their feedback.

Teachers who do leave the district should receive exit interviews that attempt to find out exactly why they decided to leave. District administrators ought to be especially interested in new teachers who leave in the first few years. What was their perception of the level of support they received? If they left teaching altogether, was their exit a result of a lack of support at the district and/or building level? These are important questions, the answers to which administrators need to know. Those who have left the profession can help the rest of us understand what changes need to be made in the overall induction system. District- and school-leadership teams need to recognize whatever departing teachers say as valuable feedback that serves continuous improvement in general and the induction program in particular.

Final Thoughts

New-teacher induction programs should be part of a larger continuous-improvement effort at the school or district level. Someone once said that if we don't model what we are teaching, then we are in danger of teaching something else entirely. An induction program that tries to push collaboration and innovation in a building that seems to value isolationism and the status quo may be less than effective to say the very least. Professional development must mean the development of *all professionals in the system,* not just those who are newly hired.

Over the years, I have seen the pressures an isolationist and largely negative school culture can bring to bear overwhelm attempts at collaboration and change. Building and district leadership must be aware of this tendency, and leadership teams should begin the process of building a shared vision that will drive change and sustain innovation over time. As stated by Zmuda and others (2004), "The beauty of continuous improvement is that it never stops, for envisioning the possibilities never ends" (p. 181). Everyone in the school community should be enlisted in discovering the possibilities for developing and retaining teachers, enhancing student performance, and creating a school culture that encourages and supports improvement efforts.

In the Prologue, Shellie's mentor was Trey, an experienced teacher, mentor, and an important player on the school's leadership team. Trey was part of a larger schoolwide commitment to Shellie, the other three new teachers, and a continuous-improvement process that encompassed the induction program. In Chapter 3, we'll examine the role of the teacher mentor as part of the overall induction program.

3

Clarity and Substance

We recently had some work done in our kitchen and foyer by an artist specializing in decorative finishing. On his first day on the job, I showed him the areas that needed work, chatted with him about how long it might take, and checked back with him once in a while to see how he was progressing. On the *second* day, having met him at the front door, I walked back to my office after saying, "Call me if you need me." This was appropriate because he knew exactly what he was doing, and there was nothing I could possibly add to his level of competence or expertise. I went back to what I had been doing safe in the knowledge he could continue without me, doing—and doing well—at what he had done a hundred times before.

Too often, teacher mentors, chosen because they "know the ropes" will familiarize new teachers with the building, introduce them to the copy room and faculty lounge, and then reduce their support to the level of "Call me if you need me." This happened to me as a new teacher, and looking back, I can see clearly how my first year was far different than it might have been had an active, formal, and effective induction program been in place. On my own back then, I charted a very conservative course that relied on students serving in the role of information receivers to my own role as information provider.

As a new teacher, I was given a teacher's edition of the textbook, an overhead projector, a blackboard, and access to tons of educational films (reel to reel); what I experienced was, I have no doubt, typical of a time when there were far more teachers than teaching positions.

With these resources and a general idea of what I ought to be doing, I proceeded through my first year as a teacher:

1. My primary instructional delivery method was lecture. I think at one point I had the overhead projector surgically attached to my hip. I often turned out the lights, turned on the projector, and revealed the notes one at a time for the edification of my ninth-graders. My students sat in neat rows and took notes (or did so only after some prodding on my part), paid attention (or faked it), and did whatever information processing they needed to do at home (or didn't).

2. I underwent a good deal of on-the-job training (OJT) in the classroom. The only thing even closely resembling a reflective conversation was with my wife after school. She was also a teacher, and we often compared notes in the evenings— something I hoped my students were doing with their parents. I knew my students had *taken* notes; I just didn't know what they *did* with them. My fantasy was that they were taking a few minutes each evening to reflect on and think deeply about what was in their notebooks. It never occurred to me that it was unlikely they had developed any real reflective capacity. I certainly had never given them time in class to reflect on the information in any collaborative sense; I was too busy "covering" the material to help them uncover it. By so doing, I sacrificed depth and understanding on the altar of breadth and speed.

3. In the faculty lounge we complained about kids that did not seem to want to learn. It never occurred to me that what they did *not* want to do was sit in neat rows, stare blankly at an overhead transparency, or process information on their own rather than find release in a thousand other more interesting things during the evening hours. I had no Trey to arrange observations of highly effective teachers and join me in the kind of reflective conversations that create knowledge and understanding out of information.

4. I had no system of self-evaluation, self-assessment, or self-reflection—only a lot of self-pity as I wondered if the teaching profession was right for me as opposed to, for example, selling real estate. I pretty much lurched uncertainly from problem to problem like a child's toy that randomly bumps into the furniture in an unpredictable, hit-or-miss way. The toy recovers or it doesn't. New teachers recover or they don't, and too often they don't.

Fortunately for me, I loved teaching, and I developed a rapport with students and faculty members alike. I was a class sponsor and yearbook adviser, and I spent long hours at the school and enjoyed it all. Looking back, I realize how much more my students and I would have benefited from the experience had there been an induction program in place. My experience may not have been unusual in the early 1970s, when teachers were a dime a dozen and human resource personnel had their pick of new and experienced teachers. This practical example of the economic law of supply and demand argued against any need for formal induction programs. My school was not unique—quite the contrary, it was just like thousands upon thousands of others in a nation where teacher vacancies were few and teachers looking to be hired to fill those vacancies were many.

In the 1980s, however, with student populations increasing rapidly and teacher shortages beginning to make an appearance, more and more school districts became interested in assisting first-year teachers in an attempt to keep them in place (Resta, 2006a, p. 103). As induction programs grew, researchers began to examine their effectiveness, and a study released in 1996 revealed that five major cities around the country, including New York and Cincinnati, managed to cut "attrition rates of beginning teachers by more than two-thirds by providing expert mentors with release time to coach beginners in their first year on the job" (National Commission on Teaching and America's Future, in Resta, 2006a, p. 103).

Understanding the Role of the Teacher Mentor

The lynchpin role of the induction program is that of the teacher mentor. For Shellie it was Trey, a trained and experienced mentor who understood his pivotal part in assisting Shellie in her growth and development as someone new to the profession. Trey worked with Shellie, safe in the assumption that his efforts on her behalf had the full support of Mr. Crandall, their principal. Trey's role as teacher mentor fit into the total professional-development picture in a school where collaboration was the norm and isolationist tendencies had been squeezed out over the course of Mr. Crandall's tenure as principal. The ongoing induction program at their middle school was part and parcel of the total continuous-improvement process.

In my experience, a great deal of frustration and confusion results when the newly hired—no matter the job—are given a title, a desk, a smile and a pat on the back—but no real understanding of exactly what it is they are supposed to do and how they are to go about doing it. More important, the newly hired may lack a big-picture vision of how they and their new task fit into the overall scheme of things. This is often true of brand new teacher mentors. Many times building administrators will ask for volunteers or simply assign a teacher who teaches the same subject and is a veteran teacher. It may be that the total training package for the new mentor amounts to "Hang in there and do the best you can for the new teacher." In these cases, it may be understandable that mentors simply look to practical ways of making the new teacher "feel right at home" in the building.

Many mentors see their jobs as making certain the new teachers know where the paper clips are stored, how many copies can be made on the machine in the office, where the bubble sheets are kept, and which numbered parking space is theirs. While all these things are important in the short run, the really critical things that get in the way of teacher growth and ultimate success have to do with instruction and process management. It is helpful if someone can get the new teacher to reflect on instruction and process-related matters. Absent a systemic approach to continuous improvement, teachers are left pretty much on their own.

Those chosen as mentors might assume that if novice teachers have a decent grounding in their subject area, along with some classroom management skills—both covered in teacher preparation programs—then some basic guidance and a few tips up front, along with a little old fashioned OJT should set new teachers up well—and the rest is up to them. This might be true for those novice teachers who are predisposed to persevere; those few who may be gifted in the art of problem solving, and who ultimately succeed no matter the odds. For the vast majority of new teachers, however, this essentially laissez-faire attitude on the part of the system can contribute to a new teacher's confusion, discouragement, and general befuddlement; the lack of active support may also lead to an early exit from the profession.

While induction programs and mentors *should* be making new teachers feel right at home in the building, the induction program's main function is to assist the new teacher in her main role—instruction. In order

---

Mentor/Protégé Focus

Mentors need to focus with their protégés on the business of classroom instruction. Teachers who experience success in the classroom, in part because of the support they get from mentors and everyone else in the building, are more likely to stay in the profession for the long haul.

for a program to have substance, everything from day one should help new teachers become confident, competent classroom instructors. This should be clear to anyone asked to become a mentor, and this emphasis on instruction should be communicated to new teachers as well. For an induction program to have substance, what happens in the classroom is critical.

As it is with the overall induction process, clarity and substance are critical components of the mentoring program. New teachers must clearly understand not only what is expected of them but also what will lead to success in the classroom. Frankly, knowledge of the nuts and bolts of the copying machine is insignificant compared to understanding which instructional and management strategies will prove successful with 30 fifth-grade students or four blocks of Algebra I. If teaching in the information age is more complex, given the technological sophistication of students at every grade level, it makes sense that the relationship between mentors and protégés is also more complex. What is expected of both the mentor and protégé should be perfectly clear, and the relationship should be one of substance—not superficiality. Novice teachers need thoughtful and meaningful support from mentors who understand their role within the overall framework of a formal induction program.

Choosing Mentors

In its simplest terms, according to Jonson (2002), mentoring "is really just one teacher facilitating the growth of another" (p. 115). Mentors who take on the responsibility of working with novice teachers need to understand that facilitating growth is no small task. It involves helping the new teacher develop a capacity for problem solving that will follow them throughout their careers. For the mentor, it means not judging the actions of a new teacher while at the same time providing encouragement and support (Jonson, 2002, pp. 110–111). Resta (2006b) reports that "Mentoring in ways that connect with beginning teachers and ultimately benefit their students requires mentors to be able to inquire sensitively, listen carefully, and look thoughtfully at their classrooms at work" (p. 198).

The growth that takes place in an effective mentor-protégé relationship is not one-sided. In a relationship that is reflective in nature, that is, where both the mentor and protégé are involved in regular conversations concerning the practice of teaching, both will benefit and both will grow. In one study, reported by Kline and Salzman

(2006), "the most effective mentors admitted that they learned as much, if not more, from their protégés as the protégés learned from them" (p. 170–171). Reflective practice is a powerful growth agent, and a mentor who year after year is actively working with protégés will benefit from the relationship—*as will their students.*

Mentoring can be a powerful professional-development opportunity, then, for mentor and protégé alike. Experienced teachers willing to commit to a substantive relationship with a new teacher can assist them and ramp up their own growth at the same time. As part of a vibrant and active schoolwide professional-development system, an effective mentoring program should serve to keep new teachers in the profession while contributing to the overall professional development of the school. If collaboration and reflective practice are already part of the fabric of school life, it follows that mentors who volunteer will be more effective with their protégés because they are already practitioners in an ongoing continuous-improvement process at the school level.

Mentors should be chosen because they are willing to commit to assisting in the professional growth of teachers, not simply because they are veterans. Experience alone does not guarantee success for a mentor-protégé relationship any more than teaching experience guarantees success for those who move from the classroom into an administrative position. Assigning mentors should not be part of a school-opening administrative checklist that also includes making certain the teacher policy manuals are done and the floors are cleaned and waxed. Thought should be given to who among the faculty will best serve the needs of a novice teacher.

If the number of novice teachers is large, and if the school district is large enough to be able to afford it, teachers can be removed from the classroom and assigned to novice teachers for up to three years. Mentors who have to worry about their own classrooms as well as those of their protégés may find the time commitment to be too burdensome, and the good work they might ordinarily do may suffer. If, as Sweeny (2002) points out, there is a conflict between the needs of the mentor's students and the needs of the protégé's students, it may be that "the students in the mentor's classroom will win, and the mentoring process and the students in the protégé's classroom will lose" (p. 20). Districts that have the resources to create a cadre of full-time mentors may well want to consider that option. Since time is a precious commodity for all teachers, mentors included, administrators may want to consider lightening the workload a bit for those members of the faculty willing to take on the vital role of mentoring new teachers.

Building-level administrators who have the responsibility of assigning mentors should make every effort to provide sufficient training; this training should be based on what is expected of mentors as they work with novice teachers. There should be a clear set of beliefs and expectations understood by prospective mentors and reinforced by training that is geared toward supporting the mentor-protégé relationships so critical to professional growth and ultimate success. Since reflective conversations are an important part of the mentor's work with new teachers, district- or buildingwide training should include instruction in how mentors can involve protégés in the kind of inquiry-based dialogue necessary for self-reflection and self-assessing.

Expectations for Mentors

Anyone in any job needs to understand what his or her duties and responsibilities are. In my experience, there is nothing more discouraging for anyone involved in education than to be unsure about what is required. In many cases, it is simply a lack of communication that brings forward movement to a grinding halt. If the mentor program is run from the district level, there need to be ongoing conversations between district- and school-level administrators concerning expectations for mentors. Any teacher who is considering becoming a mentor or is being considered for a mentor position needs to understand what the job entails—in writing. If what lies at the heart of the program is facilitating the growth of new teachers, the following should be made clear from the outset:

1. Mentors should be willing to spend a considerable amount of time with their protégés, and the administration needs to limit the number of protégés per mentor to one if possible. Part-time mentors, after all, have students of their own to whom they are responsible. Even the most energetic and dedicated mentor will flirt with burnout if the load is too heavy. Unless the district has full-time mentors, part timers have their own classes and their own lives, and this must be taken into account.

2. Mentors should also be willing to participate in a district- or school-level training program intended to develop the skill sets (facilitating reflective mentor-protégé conversations and problem-solving strategies) that will help protégés move toward becoming self-reflective, independent, and confident teacher

practitioners. New teachers need to become effective problem solvers, and mentors need to commit to making that happen, but not without the proper amount of training and support from the district and the building administration.

3. Mentors who are enthusiastic and have a consistently positive attitude will serve as powerful role models for new teachers. The growth of new teachers is likely to stagnate in the hands of mentors who are negative and hidebound in their attitudes. No one with a negative attitude should be selected as a teacher mentor, no matter how many years they have spent in the classroom. New teachers need to be around positive people. Considering the central role of the mentor in the professional development of the protégé, no one should be more positive than the mentor.

4. Mentors need to consistently model a continuous-improvement mindset. New teachers should not be paired with someone incapable of the kind of professional introspection, experimentation, and willingness to change that characterizes lifelong learners. New teachers will be observing classrooms, including those of their mentors, and they need to see teachers who are dedicated to self-reflection and relentless forward progress on behalf of kids.

5. Mentors need to display an enormous amount of empathy. This means they should reflect frequently on their first years in the profession and remember well what support they did or did not receive. I have seen mentors who are quite impatient with new teachers; getting really good in the classroom takes time, and first-year teachers are normally no less busy than veterans in the same building. They have the same demands on their time and they have the same number of students in their classes; what they don't have is the experience that will only come with time and gobs of support.

6. Finally, mentors should commit to identifying others among the faculty and staff capable and willing to assist their protégés by providing talents and strengths they themselves may not possess. If a new teacher finds herself in need of someone who is proficient in the use of electronic technology, her technologically challenged mentor can certainly find someone on staff to help. In a school where collaboration is the norm, this should not be difficult; in a school where isolationism prevails, it may

be more of a challenge, but mentors need to understand it is possible to find other faculty or staff members willing to join the effort to facilitate the growth of new teachers in the building.

Administrative Support for Mentors

We have already stressed the importance of clearly communicating to mentors their basic function and job responsibilities. There are many other ways for district and building administrators to provide support for their cadre of teacher mentors. Below are four:

1. In order to lighten the load on mentors, building administrators can find ways for the rest of the faculty and staff to support new teachers. For example, during the summer, after a principal or assistant principal has given the new teacher a tour of the building, an office associate could provide instruction in the use of essential equipment (copiers, phones, etc.). The associate could also introduce the new teacher to the head custodian and other building support personnel who are on hand during the summer.

2. So that mentors don't become overloaded or overextended, administrators can seek constantly to expand the cadre of teacher mentors. Also, the *students* of mentors actively involved in improving the teaching skills of protégés also benefit from a productive professional relationship between mentors and protégés. It follows that any principal who seeks to expand his or her mentor base is doing the smart thing. Expanding the program will improve overall instruction in the building, simply because learning between mentors and protégés is a two-way street.

3. Administrators at both the district and school level should provide training for mentors, particularly in the art of reflective conversations and coaching. The most dynamic part of the mentor-protégé relationship is that which improves instruction and makes new teachers capable of eventually facilitating their own growth by making the consistent use reflection, self-assessment, and other continuous-improvement tools routine.

4. Finally, administrators can convey a vision that allows mentors a great deal of flexibility within the general outline of their duties and responsibilities. This allows mentors to act not only

in the letter of the law, but within the spirit of the law as well. Mentors who are perceived as simply going through the motions in order to fulfill their responsibilities may be less successful with their protégés. Administrators can make it clear to mentors that being creative in pursuit of a shared vision is not just acceptable; it is encouraged. This spirit of experimentation and innovation should be valued as part of the continuous-improvement process.

For their part, districts need to provide building administrators with the research that shows the importance of new-teacher support in improving instruction and retaining those teachers in the classroom. In the school district for which I worked for 17 years, districtwide training for mentors was ongoing, with two levels of training—one for new mentors and one for veterans. No one is more attuned to the effects of teacher turnover than human resources personnel, and if there is an induction system at the school and district level, new teachers should be made aware of this before they are hired; they should enter the induction program the minute they are given a contract. It is important for new teachers to know from the outset that they will be supported in every way possible. This goes for novice teachers and experienced teachers new to the school or district.

Differentiation

There is going to be a difference in the way mentors work with novices as opposed to experienced teachers arriving at the school. Daresh (2003) points out that those teachers who arrive with experience "are probably not going to experience many problems with role identity and perhaps only limited difficulties with the technical demands of the job" (p. 66). Some difficulty in getting used to what may be a new and possibly different culture can be ameliorated by teaming that veteran teacher with a mentor. There may be a problem if the mentor is actually a good deal younger than the experienced teacher, and it may be that another experienced teacher of approximately the same age and who teaches the same subject matter might facilitate the building of a mentor-protégé relationship. It may be possible that a new teacher that is older may have absolutely no problem being paired with a younger mentor. A conversation between the administrator and the new teacher might be all that is needed to find out which pairing is best.

Facilitating Learning-Focused Conversations

The induction program at Shellie's school was part and parcel of the overall continuous-improvement model, and the entire faculty was part of this system. This made Trey's job as Shellie's mentor much easier because when he chose to speak with her about data, research, reflection, engagement strategies—these were all terms and concepts understood by a collaborative and innovative faculty. Mr. Crandall, the school's principal, made sure inservice time was not wasted on "administrivia," and instruction was the focus of small- or large-group meetings. The fact that so many teachers were continually trying new instructional strategies made it easy for Trey to find someone in-house for Shellie to observe. In that middle school, teachers spent a great deal of time looking at performance data and seeing the data results, not as threatening, but as valuable feedback. The language of the mentor-protégé relationship between Trey and Shellie was the language of the school, and there was no disconnect between the conversations they had and those at faculty and leadership team meetings.

Effective communication along these lines requires mentors to do less talking and more listening; this may be difficult for mentors who believe their job is to give new teachers good advice drawn from the deep well of wisdom and experience. This is a natural tendency in the absence of an induction system that teaches otherwise. One problem with this essentially one-sided conversation between mentor and protégé is that the latter may listen politely and then do what the context of their own background and experience tells them to do.

Mentor/Protégé Focus

Mentors would do well to listen far more than they talk when meeting with protégés. It is in the listening that solutions to problems can be found. It is in the reflection done by the protégé, and facilitated by the mentor, that real learning takes place and real progress is made. Self-reflective conversations between mentors and protégés can develop self-evaluative skills that will serve new teachers down the road.

The difficulty with advice is that is essentially just information, and it falls into the category of "telling isn't really teaching." In order for a new teacher to affect change in her classroom in a substantive way, she needs to be engaged by the mentor in a conversation that has her reflecting on her own classroom instruction or on what she has seen and heard in other classrooms. There is no other way to say this: If one person in a conversation does all the talking, the other is free to smile and nod while mentally disconnecting. In order to find out what the protégé is thinking, the mentor has to stop talking and start listening. Most teachers had speech courses in college, but how many had courses in the art of listening?

Knight (2007) notes that any book on communication has chapters related to listening. It is an essential communication skill, yet we don't seem to be very good at it. Knight puts it simply:

> We need to listen better. We know it, and yet we do not do it. We zone out of conversations, we argue with others before we fully hear what they have to tell us, and we turn the focus back to us when we should be focused on those with whom we are talking. (p. 61)

The mentor has the task of facilitating conversations with protégés, and the mentor has to learn to listen more and talk less. This may seem at odds with the idea that someone with vast experience has more to offer and share than someone new to the classroom, yet if our goal in these mentor-protégé conversations is to find out what the new teacher is doing, thinking, wondering, grappling with, confused or excited about, or upset about—listening becomes a critical tool for mentors.

Lipton and Wellman (2004) recommend the following verbal tools for anyone facilitating learning-focused conversations. These are pausing (to allow thinking), paraphrasing (to provide understanding), asking questions (to either open or focus thinking), and "extending thinking by providing resources and information" (p. 21). Notice that these tools are predicated on the assumption that the facilitator is doing less talking and more listening. For the mentor, the idea is to get the protégé fully engaged in and committed to the conversation.

In a conversation with a protégé who has just observed the classroom of an outstanding teacher, the mentor might open with, "Well, what did you see and hear during the past hour?" This open question allows the protégé a lot of latitude, and once asked, the question can be followed by a pause that first permits the protégé to think and respond. Paraphrasing on the part of the mentor can provide clarification later on, and more closed questions can help the mentor zero in on certain aspects of what the

---

Mentor/Protégé Focus

During reflective conversations between mentors and protégés, mentors can practice the twin skills of paraphrasing or asking for points of clarification. Doing this assists comprehension, and it helps avoid misunderstandings. It also models for new teachers what they should be doing in the classroom with their students. When the listener takes the time to paraphrase or otherwise clarify something, it honors the speaker.

protégé revealed about what she saw. If what she saw, for example, included two excellent strategies, the mentor can either provide or suggest a book or article that will help extend that thinking and perhaps provide instructions that will help with application should the protégé decide she wants to replicate the strategies in her classroom. In a school dedicated to the professional growth of its entire faculty, the professional-development library may contain applicable resources.

Among the ultimate goals of these reflective and facilitated conversations is to provide the mentor and the protégé with a shared understanding of where the latter is in her continuous-improvement journey. A new teacher who has just observed two or three different teachers with proven track records has the basis for comparing and contrasting what she saw with what she herself does on a daily basis. In a reflective conversation facilitated by her mentor, she has the opportunity to think out loud about how what she observed informs and affects her own practice. The mentor has the satisfaction of knowing that his scheduling of the classroom observations, along with his reflective and learning-focused follow-up conversations, had the effect of improving instruction in the protégé's classroom—and in his own.

Final Thoughts

Choosing and training teacher mentors is no small matter, and district and building administrators need to work backward from a vision of what the role of the mentor is within the overall induction system, followed by arriving at an understanding of exactly what the role of the induction program may be within the structure of the larger professional-development program. It is critical that administrators provide the kind of clarity that will allow mentors to operate freely and smoothly. Mentors must also understand that the position is one of substance, not superficiality.

According to Jonson (2002), the qualitative nature of the relationship between mentor and protégé is more critical to ultimate success than the program's goals or activities (p. 9). Every veteran teacher had a first year and may well have experienced a few days or weeks wondering what might lie ahead and what teaching at this particular school would be like. This anxiety can be alleviated with a phone call on the part of a mentor who begins the relationship-building process early on and continues with its development as the year progresses. In Chapter 4, we'll look at ways to ramp up important relationships in the name of continuous improvement.

4

Ramping Up Relationships

One of Mr. Crandall's first tasks as a new principal, years before Shellie was hired, was to create a safe climate where collaboration could thrive. Teachers, along with the rest of the staff, learned over time they could trust their principal and that he would not betray that trust. Mr. Crandall did not play the blame game, and he was quick to accept responsibility for his own miscalculations and mistakes. He also spent a good deal of time training teacher mentors, and he modeled with the entire staff the kind of reflective dialogue he expected them to use with all new teachers. He walked the talk, and this was not lost on the staff. The faculty and administration operated within the principles of a shared vision, and the induction program was simply part of that entire system of continuous improvement.

Ten years prior to Shellie's hiring, Trey had come to the middle school as a second-year teacher who quickly came to understand with some clarity the difference between his first year of teaching—with its total lack of support and any hint of collaboration—and his first year with Mr. Crandall in a school dedicated to student and teacher success. Few at his first school had attempted relationship building at anything above a personal level. Trey had retreated into himself; he dealt with problems and crises as best he could; and he nearly quit. The difference between the two schools became apparent as soon as he was hired. His mentor at the new school was Mimi Slattery, an English teacher, and she quickly established both a personal and professional relationship that not only made Trey feel at home but also helped him focus on management and instruction from the beginning. Mimi Slattery was his official mentor for two years, during which time Trey flourished in a way that would have been impossible in his first year of teaching at the other school.

After her interview at the middle school, Shellie knew this was where she wanted to teach. Late one afternoon, she received a call from Mr. Crandall, informing her she would be the new social studies teacher on the Cardinal team. Mr. Crandall's phone call initiated the relationship building with Shellie, and each of the other three new teachers eventually received that first phone call from Mr. Crandall as principal of the school. He arranged with the district's human resources office for them to contact him first so that he could call his new teachers personally.

The second voice Shellie heard later that evening was Trey's, and he set up a time for them to meet at school. He arranged for her to talk not only with him but with the Cardinal team members as well, including the social studies teacher who was moving with her husband to another city. Moving quickly, Mr. Crandall and Trey wanted to begin the process of making Shellie feel welcome. New teachers who are handed the keys to their classrooms, given a hundred student textbooks, and told, "My door is always open!" have just been volunteered for the sink-or-swim induction model. Mr. Crandall understood that, and made sure he and his leadership team communicated early and often with new employees, including those in support roles.

Professional Relationships

While the development of personal relationships is important, it is the professional relationship between mentor and protégé that will ultimately guide the new teacher along his or her own continuous-improvement path. This professional relationship is developed through meetings where mentors and their protégés can reflect on what makes teachers effective, along with what makes learning stick. Even novice teachers are veteran students, and as such, they know a good deal

Mentor/Protégé Focus

New teachers already have a wealth of knowledge about how students learn, and about how great teachers teach. Mentors can tap into that depth and breadth of existing knowledge in order to surface observations, insights, and beliefs that will not only help inform the thinking of protégés, but will lead them to valuable applications.

about what works in classrooms. New teachers can use this considerable experience to inform their own thinking about what might be most effective in their own teaching.

Mentors can and should help teachers tap into this wealth of prior knowledge. If the breadth and depth of the mentor's *own* experience as teacher and learner is added into the mix, reflective conversations facilitated by the mentor can surface insights that will enhance the collective wisdom of mentor and protégé alike. Lipton and Wellman (2005) affirm that "By facilitating a professional vision, skillful mentors support novice teachers in clarifying and articulating the values and beliefs that drive their practice" (p. 153). Skilled mentors, according to Lipton and Wellman, continue "to enlarge the professional landscape by helping to prioritize tasks and identifying the various types of resources needed to support goal achievement" (p. 153). Mentors and protégés can thus form a powerful and dynamic professional relationship that will benefit them both and at the same time enhance learning in their classrooms.

It is during those conversations about teaching and learning that mentors can help new teachers get into the habit of reflective thinking. It is by looking at *how* and *why* we do *what* we do that we can make the adjustments we need to make in order to improve. A new teacher who feels she can be open and honest with her mentor then needs to learn to be open and honest with herself about what *is* and *is not* working in the classroom. This involves taking a close look at "what students are doing and thinking, and how instruction has been understood and embraced as classes unfold" (Bartell, 2005, p. 138). When teachers observe other classes, they can get into the habit of observing students closely, paying attention to the message delivered by body language and facial expressions. In their own classes, teachers should get in the habit of observing *their own* students when they are engaged in tasks or activities.

The kinds of reflective conversations that take place between mentors and protégés can serve as a model for discussions with students about the nature of teaching and learning. I always remind teachers that students are veterans; a sophomore is in his eleventh year of school and has some clearly defined ideas about how he learns best, along with what instructional methodology is more (or less) effective. Realizing that all students learn in different ways makes a classroom discussion about learning styles particularly relevant. I have found that students enjoy talking about how they best process, understand, and retain information. Knowing exactly what the teacher is trying to accomplish, along with how she intends to do it, goes a long way toward tapping into the shared vision of the schoolhouse.

This kind of classroom collaboration is less likely to happen, however, unless the same safe climate—composed of trust, openness, and honesty—that exists between mentor and protégé has become the norm at the classroom level. Teachers must understand that students will not take the risks necessary to improve if it is not safe to do so within the confines of that classroom. For example, students will not ask questions or volunteer answers freely if they risk being laughed at by their peers or deal with sarcasm from students or teachers. In Chapter 5, we will examine the importance of planning, and no reflective conversation is more important than the one concerning teacher-student relationships and the creation of a classroom environment that makes effective student interaction and collaboration possible.

Enlisting Modeling as a Tool

Everything we see or hear or experience provides more context for later reflection and discussion. Mentors and building administrators need to make certain that new teachers get to see great teachers teach. It is one thing to *list* the qualities of highly effective teachers; it is quite another to see them in action and observe closely how they manage process with 30 ninth graders. New teachers need to spend a good deal of time in the classrooms of effective teachers, and mentors should follow close on the heels of these observations with reflective conversations uninterrupted by the normal "busyness" of school life. These discussions are best served when mentors and protégés make sure interruptions are eliminated or kept to a minimum.

> ### Mentor/Protégé Focus
>
> When protégés observe other classrooms, mentors can help them determine in advance what one or two things they will look for during the observation. The area of focus can be determined in a pre-observation meeting between the protégé and the teacher being observed. Doing this can help the classroom teacher as much as the protégé; it will give them some feedback concerning, for example, the amount of wait time that follows a question asked by the teacher.

Mentors also need to be open about letting protégés observe their own classes. This may be doubly effective if the mentor teaches the same subject and if, as should be the case, the mentor models the kind of instruction that engages students and gets proven and consistent results. My suggestion is that mentors tell protégés to look for one or two things during the classroom visit. First, for example, the protégé might spend the period observing the students (not the teacher) in order to gauge their reactions to whatever is happening in the classroom. Second, the mentor might have the protégé determine whether the students seem to feel comfortable with sharing, asking questions, or answering them. This classroom observation might be followed by a reflective conversation that focuses on the observations of both mentor and protégé, and it should serve as a rich source of feedback for both.

Below are some questions that mentors can pose to protégés who have just observed the classroom of other teachers. They are, in fact, among questions that might be provided to new teachers before the classroom visit. Having these questions in advance allows a new teacher to focus on instruction rather than on peripheral matters (bulletin boards, wall posters, etc.). There are many more possible questions, but here are a few:

- Did it appear that the body language of students indicated that they were fully engaged? If they were, what did you see or hear that may have caused them to be engaged?
- Did the teacher provide wait time after asking a question of the class, and if so, approximately how many seconds were provided? Is there an advantage to providing more wait time after asking a question or before indicating to the class that an answer provided by a student is correct or incorrect?
- Did the teacher provide for students to process information in pairs, trios, or groups? How might providing those processing opportunities benefit students?
- Were students provided with time to stand and move about the room in order to conduct student-to-student discussions or other planned interactions? If so, what purpose might movement serve in the classroom environment?
- Did the classroom seem to be set up to facilitate the movement of teacher and students? What kind of furniture configuration would make paired or group interaction possible—either seated or standing?

Having these questions in advance can make for some great follow-up conversations between mentors and protégés. For example, one important discussion should center on this question: What constitutes engagement on the part of students? Students who spend 30 minutes cutting various shapes out of construction paper so they can get to a truly engaging lesson using those shapes might be better served by a teacher who brings the shapes to class precut and ready to go. This is a great opportunity for a mentor to have a discussion with a protégé about the difference between *engagement* and *busyness,* and the relative educational impact of both. It is important to note that simply *telling* a new teacher the difference between the two is less effective than facilitating its discovery on the part of the protégé as part of a reflective conversation.

If there are several new teachers in a building, all the mentors and protégés could certainly get together following a series of classroom observations to reflect as a group on what they saw and heard, as well as what the implications might be for their own classrooms concerning what they observed. Bringing more teachers into the discussion, I have found, increases the number of perspectives and may make for a deeper and more impactful conversation. Two teachers who observed the same classroom at the same time may have seen, heard, or understood different things. With six or eight total teachers involved in the discussion, one mentor can serve as process facilitator to keep everyone on track.

Mentors Modeling Great Lessons

Mentors can also model lessons in the new teacher's classroom. One of the most effective teacher coaches I ever met spent several years as a full-time teacher coach at the middle and high school level. Teachers who observed her teach often doubted their own students would respond to strategies intended to engage them deeply in the learning process. The excuses came at a rapid rate as teachers explained that *their own* students were too antsy, too slow, too this, and too that. These teachers often became believers after seeing this teacher coach do exactly what the teachers had come to believe could not be done— *and with their students*. This teacher coach did not simply suggest this or that strategy or technique; it was her job to spend time in those classrooms walking the talk and then facilitating reflective conversations that very often resulted in a new shared vision of what can be done if teachers are willing to take risks and then reflect on process.

One of the most effective mentors I have ever met was a businessman, not a teacher, yet by his actions he facilitated my own professional growth and caused me to forever see him as a superb leader and coach. This man, Paul Elchynski, was the owner and manager of a supermarket in the small town in which I grew up. I was then between my freshman and sophomore year in high school, and this was my first job. Most days after school, I would report to the super-market prepared to bag groceries and carry them to the customers' cars. I can still clearly remember my first day at work, standing at the end of the belt as groceries cascaded toward me at what seemed a dizzying pace.

Paul stood right next to me, opened a bag (they were all *paper* bags in 1965), and began to model process. As he packed the bag he talked about placing the heavy items in the bottom, squaring the sides of the bags with rectangular boxes, and topping it all off with light items and eggs. He also explained that cold items should always be placed in the same bag. Finally, having filled the last of several bags on a big order, he and I accompanied the customer to her car while he talked with her. He knew her name; I discovered he knew most of his customers by name, and he taught me to learn them as well.

When I finally opened a bag and began working on a large order, he opened one as well and gave me running feedback until I felt com-fortable with the task. By the end of my first day on the job—the day before Thanksgiving—I was able to hold my own in the busiest lines, and I loved every minute of it because I knew what I was doing. He did not tell me what to do and then walk away; he did not lecture me on the fine points of bagging as we sat in his office; and he was an outstanding teacher and mentor. He modeled bagging groceries, and I watched. Then he modeled while I practiced. He gave me immedi-ate feedback during the process, and because of that, I was able to make necessary adjustments along the way.

What I was supposed to do became crystal clear to me after only an hour or so, but there was something else this owner/manager/teacher did. As we returned with an empty cart from the parking lot, he had me observe the way he talked to customers, and his commitment to service began to resonate with me. Over the days, weeks, and months beginning that Thanksgiving weekend, he shared his vision with me, as he did with the entire staff. We bought into the fact that we were not just bagging groceries or stocking shelves or cleaning floors or running cash registers; we were building lasting relationships with the people of our small town.

Within a few years, this three-supermarket town had become a one-supermarket town, and it was not pricing or better loaves of bread that did it. It was the vision of one man, shared by those of us lucky enough to share it, that made the dream reality. After gradua-tion, I came back during the summer and over short breaks from col-lege to work in the supermarket, and to this day his approach to *building relationships with employees and customers alike* has stayed with me; and over many decades, it has continued to provide me with many valuable lessons. He understood that we were not selling groceries; we were selling service. We were *building relationships* that led to success on many levels. Teacher mentors should take the time to build professional relationships with protégés that will pave the way for ultimate success.

The Importance of Climate

Mentors can perhaps find no better reflective conversation to have with new teachers than that concerning classroom climate and the continuous effort to cultivate personal and professional relationships with students. Once again, even teachers who have little teaching experience are veteran students, and they have spent many years observing teachers, professors, and their own classmates as they react to whatever happens in the classroom. This considerable depth of knowledge can be plumbed by the mentor as he or she attempts to surface prior knowledge about the importance of a safe classroom climate and solid, positive relationships. This conversation can also be the perfect time to discuss the importance of enlisting the support of students in pursuing common classroom goals.

A brand new teacher, even one just out of college, can reach back into his or her past and surface plenty of stories about teachers or professors who did or did not do what was necessary to establish and maintain a positive classroom atmosphere that encourages students to take risks. When involved in such conversations, the mentor who relies exclusively on her own past for insight may miss the chance to get the protégé thinking deeply about his own personal experiences and the valuable insights available there. It is far more helpful for mentors and protégés to arrive at what may be a set of *shared beliefs* about what makes a classroom safe for risk taking on the part of students. Protégés will appreciate being part of the conversation rather than the recipient of yet another piece of well-meaning advice. In this kind of reflective conversation, it is ultimately the insight provided by the new teacher that may carry the most weight.

My experience after such conversations with teachers is that body language, facial expressions, and tone of voice often surface as factors for creating safe classroom environments. New (or veteran) teachers have a ready list of their own teachers whose body language and facial expressions betrayed a grumpy demeanor or perpetually negative attitude that kept kids in a state of fear, or at the very least inhibited the kind of healthy student-teacher or student-to-student interactions that are necessary for the learning process to take root and grow. Letting new teachers once again touch base with their own emotions will almost certainly pave the way for a conversation facilitated by the mentor about how this ultimately might affect the protégé's own classroom. Having recognized and verbalized that a safe and positive classroom climate is an integral component of the continuous-improvement process, mentor and protégé can work together on what needs to be done to make that happen.

A discussion about teachers in the protégé's past who may have been negative and those who have been supremely positive begs the question *do words matter?* The short and inescapable answer is, of course, yes. Denton (2008) affirms that language can be a force for good or bad. Words can "lift students to their highest potential or tear them down" (p. 28). Denton goes on to say that language can help teachers either "build positive relationships or encourage discord and distrust" (p. 28). This is as true of relationship building in the classroom as it is in the building of relationships between mentors and their protégés. Mentors must be positive role models, and they must choose with great care the language they use as they facilitate the kinds of reflective conversations during which they want new teachers to open up and willingly share and contribute.

One effective tool in the arsenal of one trying to build and sustain relationships is silence. Denton (2008) stresses the need for teachers to use silence, thus giving students time to process information before making a decision as to whether to share. Mentors can model this by giving protégés time to think and collect their thoughts before beginning the conversation. Listening is a complex skill; in spite of its importance, and even though "we spend 55 percent of our lives listening," according to Costa (2008), "it is one of the least taught skills in schools" (p. 33). In the same way a teacher should not be perceived by students as simply *composing his next sentence* while a student talks, mentors need to truly listen as their protégés talk. Costa calls this generative listening—"the art of developing deeper silences in yourself, so you can slow your mind's hearing to your ears' natural speed and hear beneath the words to their meaning" (p. 33).

Mentor/Protégé Focus

Mentors can make certain that plenty of time is set aside for conversations with protégés. New teachers not only have a great deal to learn; they also have a great deal to share. Mentors can serve the cause of continuous improvement by being good listeners.

During reflective conversations, mentors need to listen, pause, and paraphrase in order to seek clarity and make certain both discussion partners are on the same sheet of music.

A certain amount of mentor-protégé communication can take place using e-mail, but my preference is still for face-to-face conversations, the modeling of which will serve teachers well in their own practice. Jonson (2002) looks at it from the standpoint of the new teacher: "Perhaps the best way to reflect—the most productive—is out loud, talking with a mentor or peer" (p. 115). I would also suggest that *plenty of time be set aside* for these conversations. These kinds of cognitive conversations cannot take place on the cheap, and they should not be held in the hallway between classes. When they do take place, it should be with the understanding that they will be free of interruptions. If the mentor realizes the amount of time originally allotted is not going to be nearly enough, it is far better to simply reschedule the conversation for another day or time.

A Matter of Trust

One element that is critical in developing relationships between mentors and their protégés is trust. Confidentiality is a hallmark of that trust, and new teachers must know that mentors will not consider what is said in mentor-protégé conferences as fodder for water-fountain gossip. It will not do for the protégé to hear something shared with the mentor yesterday repeated in the faculty lounge today. Hearing something like this would most certainly have a negative effect on the relationship. In addition, Jonson (2002) states that mentors must "demonstrate openness, honesty, and candor," and they should not "hide behind the cloak of bureaucratic power and seniority" (p. 109). A new teacher, who is already apprehensive about what she will face in the classroom and in the school community at large, needs to know from the outset that in her mentor she has someone who will earn the trust she wants to place in him.

Climate and Trust Issues at the Building Level

Administrators have an important role to play in encouraging that sense of trust between mentors and new teachers by engendering a climate of trust in the school as a whole. The mentor's role is made more difficult if the general atmosphere of the building is not conducive to collaboration. In short, and in the words of Bartell (2005), administrators must foster a climate "in which the dialogue between new teacher and mentor can occur most productively" (p. 50). Bartell says one thing administrators can do is to make certain that "site-level activities related to the induction program take place" (p. 50). The mentor program is only as successful as the overall induction program of which it is a component. From the standpoint of the mentors, if the perception is that the administration is not fully committed to the induction program as a whole, this creates problems for the mentoring program. If mentor-training sessions that are scheduled, for example, do not take place and are not rescheduled—this lack of support for the program is likely to negatively impact mentors and protégés alike. They must be able to trust administrators to follow through on commitments related to training and other professional-development opportunities. Things that are scheduled to happen and subsequently don't happen will begin to tear at the fabric of the school community, and reduce the amount of trust that is necessary to get the job done in the classroom.

Bobek (2001) gives lack of administrative support as a primary reason why teachers leave the profession. This underscores the role of administrators in committing to constructing a solid foundation of positive relationships within the school community. Teachers (new or otherwise) and administrators, according to Bobek, need to have "respect for one another's roles and a willingness to listen and to learn from one another" on the way to a healthy and positive environment (p. 203). This kind of school climate can go far toward encouraging and sustaining effective mentor-protégé relationships.

Final Thoughts

Over the years, I have seen mentors whose relationship with their protégés went far beyond the official partnership obligation of one or two years. Some have become fast friends, while others barely speak to each other. Among the variables that affect the relationships between mentors and protégés, as we have seen, is trust. Once betrayed, those relationships may be lost. This may happen early in the official mentor-protégé partnership, and it may be something about which administrators are totally unaware. Earlier, I said that mentors should not be chosen simply because they teach the same subject as the new teacher nor because they know the ropes in the building. A mentor who is consistently unable to develop proper and effective relationships in the classroom is not likely to develop positive and powerful relationships with teachers.

Not everyone is *naturally* capable of developing relationships with everyone with whom they come into contact. However, the kinds of skills we talked about in this and other chapters—active listening, for example—can be taught to those who would otherwise like to be mentors. District- and building-level professional-development programs should include this essential training for potential mentors. Ongoing training should be able to provide a pool of possible mentors and will also build leadership capacity in the building or school district as a whole.

Thoughtful, purposeful, and reflective planning is a critical component for continuous improvement in the schoolhouse. Too many new teachers walk into their classrooms and find themselves reacting to things they did not see coming. Once new teachers get into a largely reactive mode, their own confidence may begin to wane as they see themselves as incompetent and, if they begin to play the blame game, victims. Many promising careers have been short-circuited early on due to a lack of planning. In Chapter 5, we'll take a look at ways mentors can help protégés on process-management issues that may make the difference come November or December.

5

A Place for Everything

While a brand new eighth-grade language arts teacher may be relatively inexperienced when it comes to running a classroom, her students are grizzled veterans. Eighth graders are in their ninth year of formal schooling, and they have seen it all: dozens of teachers and pounds of textbooks and worksheets, with rules and procedures by the score. In the first month of school, these veterans size up this new group of teachers, asking the same silent questions they pose every year: *Will this teacher try to get to know me? How will she deal with tardies? What are her restroom policies? Will she lecture most of the time? Will she take weeks to return tests? Will she lose her temper? If she calls only on those with their hands raised, will that give me a pass when it comes to class discussion?* The context within which these questions are raised is the experience of each student; if they talk at lunch about this new group of teachers (and they do), then their collective experience comes into play as they compare, contrast, infer, and draw conclusions about what lies ahead.

Before too many weeks have passed, students are beginning to act and react in class based on what they are learning about this new teacher, and the patterns of student behavior developed over many years begin to surface in class. For novice teachers who thought that September was both wonderful and a harbinger of things to come, these behaviors cause them to react as each situation presents itself. Bereft of the big-picture view that experience often brings, and lacking guidance and support from their administrators and colleagues, new teachers begin to spend many long evenings doubting their own reactions and approaches to problems that seem to be multiplying and increasing in severity. *They begin to question their own competence.*

Students are nothing if not perceptive, and a student who has been in school a number of years knows a well-run classroom when he sees it. He also knows when a teacher—especially a novice teacher—seems to be reacting (and overreacting) to events, rather than executing a deliberate and solid plan. The fact is that a newly hired teacher who has little in the way of classroom experience simply does not have the capacity to zoom out and see where in the big scheme of things all the management components fit. They may know that procedures are important; are they clear on how much time is needed to turn procedures into routines? They may get that they need to facilitate student-to-student discussions in the classroom; are they aware that unless students practice by discussing things familiar to them, they will not be comfortable jumping into content-laden conversations? Finally, they may truly believe that building relationships with students and parents is critical; do they understand that developing those relationships begins—before the kids report on the first day of school—with initial phone calls in August?

Pulling Back for a Larger View

Today, through the magic of Google, we can see planet Earth from above, looking at a particular geographic area in incredible detail or zooming out to get a big-picture view. That larger view can provide context and meaning for the close-up shots. For example, the spectacle of acre after acre of grapes may make more sense when we zoom out and notice that those grapes are located on the shores of Lake Erie—a climate perfectly suited to growing concord grapes. The large fruit-processing facility in the midst of these grape vineyards now makes much more sense, as do a large number of sweet and sour cherry orchards. Within the larger context of the climate in that region of the country, the location of orchards, vineyards, and fruit-processing plants, along with an increasing number of vintners makes perfect sense. As we zoom out, courtesy of the satellites orbiting overhead, myriad elements come together to present a more complete and more understandable picture.

Novice teachers, lacking in experience and unable to zoom out using the reflective lens our veteran teachers possess, are often hired in the spring or early summer to teach a grade or subject, and then spend the rest of the summer relaxing and wondering what it will be like having their own classrooms. Too many new teachers spend only that one inservice week in the building putting up bulletin boards, listening to talking heads expounding on everything from insurance to policy-manual changes, and trying to make sense of schedules. Curriculum guides are a mystery, as are the hundred or so textbooks delivered during lunch one day.

Four or five inservice days go by in a rush and soon it is time to meet the students. A good many single and seemingly disparate tasks have been taken care of during that week, and office-generated checklists have been completed. That one week before the students report is often so jam packed with administrivia that it does not provide new teachers with the time to think about, grapple with, and ask questions about what lies ahead.

There is a place for everything in teaching. Mentors have a place in providing a foundation for success for teachers new to the profession is as soon as teachers are officially hired. Mentors can also help provide that big-picture view their experience provides. New teachers sometimes don't know what questions to ask or what questions are most important. By spending some time with his or her protégé during the summer, a teacher mentor can begin to develop a relationship that will allow for the kind of interaction that will serve the relationship well. There is no time to waste over the summer months for the simple reason that, left to their own devices, new teachers will, predictably, focus on how their classroom looks and how the copy machine works. These are things that, while necessary, should be placed in the larger context of those components of planning that are critical to success in the short run, things that contribute to a long and successful career, rather than to a turbulent—and too often short—career.

> ### Mentor/Protégé Focus
>
> If a mentor has the luxury of knowing in the late spring or early summer that a new teacher has been officially hired, he or she should waste no time in meeting with that protégé. A great deal can be accomplished before the teachers report in August.

If new teachers are hired in the spring for a fall start, and if there is time remaining in the school year, my suggestion is that teacher mentors and administrators arrange for the new teacher to visit two or three absolutely superb classrooms where students are consistently and deeply engaged in the learning process; where procedures have become routine; and where it is obvious that mutual respect has helped create an environment in which students are not afraid to take risks, ask questions, and collaborate. In each case, new teachers can be instructed to observe the students—not the teacher—for much of the class period, perhaps answering the following questions as they relate to students:

- What does their body language betray about their level of engagement?
- If they are working in pairs or groups, are they on task for most of the time?
- Is their overall level of comfort in that classroom high?
- Did the classroom seem to function smoothly, with little time wasted?

Once the observations are completed, the mentor and his protégé can take the time to reflect on what she noticed as she visited those classes. There may be a temptation on the part of the mentor to *explain* why things ran smoothly, why kids were engaged, and why the level of respect seemed high. Rather than offering explanations or even advice (which may be rejected for any number of reasons), this is the time for what Lipton and Wellman (2004) call inquiry intended "to support a colleague in exploring issues, problems, concerns and ideas" (p. 58). The inquiry that follow a classroom observation can involve open-ended questions that serve as "an *invitation* to engage and think" (p. 58). The classroom observations (complete with notes and written reflections), along with subsequent inquiry-based conversations with the mentor can provide the protégé with some context within which what she observed, contemplated, wrestled with—and ultimately, perhaps, concluded—may make sense.

According to Lipton and Wellman (2004), there are three reflective stages that can serve to lead the new teacher to new connections and understandings about why the classrooms she observed seemed to be safe, inviting, and productive places. The three stages are listed below, along with examples of post-observation questions that serve to help mentor and protégé understand the implications of what the latter observed in those classrooms:

1. *Activating and Engaging* (opening the reflective conversation)
   - What did you notice as you observed the students in those classes?
   - Is there anything else you would like to talk about related to what you observed?

2. *Exploring and Discovering* (time to uncover what might have caused those behaviors)

   - Among those things you observed, what really stood out?
   - What sequence of events may have led to what you observed?

3. *Organizing and Integrating* (bringing the discussion home to the application level)

   - What did you see that may influence how you approach teaching in general and planning in particular?
   - Based on what you saw in your classroom observations, what advice might you give other teachers? (adapted from Lipton & Wellman, 2004)

Providing the context for a reflective discussion between the mentor and the protégé paves the way for the latter to discover on her own that well-run, engaging, and productive classrooms don't just happen. Great teachers don't introduce content so quickly that they forget to turn procedures into routines, develop powerful relationships, and create a classroom environment that can support the introduction of course content a few days or more into the school year. Everything has its place in the planning process, *and mastering process before introducing content is essential to success.* Teachers who jump into the subject-area curriculum too quickly may encounter obstacles later on when students are increasingly unclear as to what is expected of them.

> ### Mentor/Protégé Focus
>
> New teachers may be so intent on course content that they may not pay enough attention to process. Every procedure (the way the students come into the room, how the teacher gets their attention, how they are dismissed, etc.) that becomes routine during the first two weeks will contribute to ultimate success. Mentors can emphasize the importance of putting the process horse in front of the content cart.

In the classrooms of teachers who spend the first week of school establishing a strong procedural framework, things tend to run far more smoothly all year long. A brand new teacher who observes two or three excellent and high-performing classrooms, taking notes and focusing on certain things, is in a position—with the help of a teacher mentor—to come to some conclusions about how his classroom should run. Once again, the observations, followed by the reflective discussion, allow the new teacher a glimpse into classroom environments conducive to learning. Having seen the best, they can subsequently reflect on what made them so, with application possibilities that came, not from advice from someone else, but from their own minds as they observed, reflected, *and came to some conclusions of their own* about what their classrooms might look like, sound like, and feel like.

All this is not to suggest that at Mr. Crandall's school Shellie did not need to know the location of the office supplies or the media center's usage guidelines. The focus of any induction program needs to be on planning and instruction, areas that increase the likelihood of success; Mr. Crandall and Trey, Shellie's mentor, clearly understood that. From the day after Shellie was hired, the induction system at her middle school shifted into gear, and she was able to visit two classrooms, one in another school district. The veteran teachers Shellie observed understood the role that student engagement, high expectations, powerful relationships, and continuous improvement play in student success. Trey and Shellie met after those classroom visits; and through his questioning and her thoughtful reflection, he facilitated Shellie's understanding of what she had seen, along with what implications it had for her own classroom.

We have already suggested that new teachers (all teachers, for that matter) should call parents as soon as they have their class lists, beginning the relationship-building process before the first day of school. When I taught on the inclusion team in middle school, I started making calls on the Thursday before school began, and I continued through the weekend. With over a hundred students, I was admittedly unable to finish before the students arrived for the first day of school; and during that first week I had my seventh graders coming up to me and asking when I would be calling *their* parents. I realized that they wanted me to call their homes because they had heard from their classmates that these were "good" phone calls. Often, the only calls parents get are those that presage some punishment for a breach of discipline at school. Those calls got me off to a great start with parents and guardians, and that investment served me—and my students—well.

By the time Shellie's students reported on the first day of school, she had accomplished much. The classroom observations arranged by Trey, along with the subsequent reflective conversations, had caused her to think carefully about the relative importance of process and content. During the summer, as we have seen, the custodians cleaned the rooms of all four new teachers first. This enabled these new teachers to spend some time getting used to their new surroundings, and Shellie rearranged her furniture based on what she had seen in one of the two middle school classes she had observed. Her arrangement is identical to that in Figure 5.1.

Figure 5.1   Perimeter Furniture Arrangement

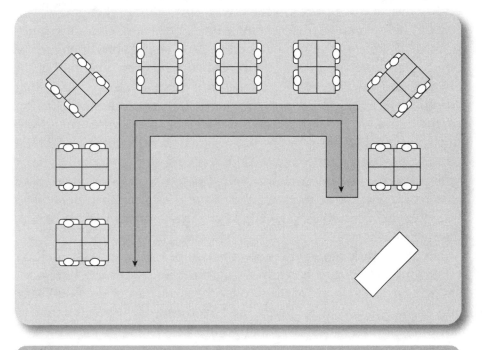

Created by Brian T. Jones

This arrangement allowed her students to talk in pairs (shoulder to shoulder or across the tables) or work in quartets. Also, it facilitated movement and student-to-student discussions while they stood in pairs or trios. She moved her teacher's desk from front and center to a corner, allowing for even more freedom of movement within the classroom.

Having moved the furniture, Shellie stood in the front of her classroom and realized that if she moved up and level with the second group of student desks, everyone could see her and no one had his or her back to her. She would instruct them to shift slightly to face her, so that with little fuss she could arrange it so she could establish eye contact with them. She also sat at enough student desks to determine that they would have a clear view of the screen when she used it. This furniture arrangement also made it possible for her to move efficiently from group to group while always being close to the farthest students in the pairs or quartets. One of the teachers she had observed had tennis balls on the chair and desk legs in order to facilitate the quiet movement of the furniture, and she made a mental note to find out how she could get her hands on a large supply of tennis balls.

Knowing she would be in school that summer day, Trey had left on her desk a three-page checklist with several housekeeping items. It included a map of the school, with several key locations highlighted. The second page contained step-by-step instructions for the two copiers in the building. The third sheet contained the number for an assigned parking space, along with several other things that would make her life easier but did not require much thought. On top of the handout he had placed two books that were gifts from Mr. Crandall and the school's professional-development leadership team. One dealt with brain-based learning and the other was a well-respected classroom management book; both were given to all new teachers at the school, and they were books that had been used last year in book clubs facilitated by central office middle school instructional coaches.

By the middle of the afternoon on that mid-summer day, Shellie's classroom was physically ready. After sitting and looking at her notes, she resolved to call one of the two teachers she had observed in May and ask a few questions. Shellie and Trey had discussed the importance of the first week of school with students in establishing and practicing classroom procedures so that they became routine. Shellie had noticed with surprise that this particular teacher had played a song on her CD player when it was time to clean up the desks and get ready to go. Shellie had been sitting in a group of four students when the music had started, and she had to move as the seventh graders had begun to put materials away, clean the desk tops, and stack their books on top of the desk prior to the change of classes. When the bell rang, students stayed in place until the opening notes of *Hit the Road, Jack*, by Ray Charles, signaled it was time to go. On cue, the students stood and began to leave. She stood at the door and said goodbye as they sort of "grooved" out the door to the accompaniment of the music. When they were gone, the teacher used her remote to stop that piece of music, at which point she cued up another song for the benefit of the students entering the room for the next class.

Shellie wanted to learn more about the use of music, and she wanted to pick the teacher's brain about what the first week of school looked like in her classroom. Trey and Shellie had discussed many things related to that first week of school, and she looked forward to talking to this master teacher about why and how things ran so smoothly in her seventh-grade classroom. She was pretty certain by now that one big key to her ultimate success lay in that first week with kids. She promised to come up with a plan for that first five days that would make the rest of the year far more effective and pre-

> ### Mentor/Protégé Focus
>
> Among the questions mentors can have protégés answer as they observe superb teachers in action might be the following: Does the class seem to run smoothly in terms of processes? A post-observation conversation between the protégé and the teacher he observed can reveal much about how important the first two weeks of school are as it relates to process.

dictable. Trey, Mr. Crandall, and her own Cardinal teammates had all emphasized the critical importance of that first week, and Shellie was beginning to understand why.

Wong and Wong (2005) drive home the point, clearly articulating that a teacher's ultimate success during the school year is dependent on what he or she "does or does not do" in the first days of school (p. 1). It is the difference between choosing to be proactive as a teacher or accepting a reactive role. Mentors who concentrate on what needs to be done during that first week of school are contributing to the new teachers' ultimate success.

First Things First

Below are some suggestions as to what can be done during those first few days in order to set the tone and provide the structural framework for the rest of the year.

Learn names quickly

When I was an instructional coordinator and an organizational development specialist with the Virginia Beach City Public Schools, central office personnel were required to substitute in the schools five days per school year. Having taught for two years on a middle school inclusion team, I really got to enjoy working with kids with learning disabilities; and whenever possible, I would seek out opportunities to substitute for those teachers. At the elementary level, the students' names were often written on cards permanently affixed to the desks. As soon as the kids were involved in an assignment, I moved around the classroom and began to memorize their names.

In a few minutes, I had them cover up their names on the desks as I spoke each of their names in turn. The effect was always the same—they loved it. Learning and using their names quickly was an effective first step at creating rapport, even in my role as a substitute for only one or two days. During five years of training substitute teachers, I modeled this as a way of building rapport. I once had a new substitute teacher call me to say he had done this with four classes of middle school students, and he had no problems for the three days he spent with them as a substitute.

On the very first day of school, teachers can have students make name tents out of 3" × 5" index cards and keep them there until the teacher is confident he or she has the names memorized. Teachers can find out early whether kids have nicknames, and they can use them. If a student or workshop participant answers a question, I will say, "So, Randy, you are saying that . . . ," and then, "Thank you for sharing, Randy." I say his name one more time in my mind, and then I move on, having used the name twice out loud and at least once silently in order to shift it from short-term to long-term memory. The more you use someone's name, the better chance you have of remembering it. Again, both students and adults appreciate the teacher's effort and commitment to doing this.

Practice procedures until they become routine

Any high school junior has been in scores of classrooms over the course of his or her student career. Common sense tells me that there are many classroom procedures for getting up to sharpen a pencil, hand in homework, clean up or line up, or to get ready at the start of a class period. Getting up to sharpen a pencil in one class may be as simple as going to the sharpener whenever one needs to, while in another class holding the pencil up is the desired cue. Yet another teacher may have a glass full of pencils he simply holds out to someone who just broke his own pencil point, while another requires students to have two sharpened pencils at all times and does not allow students to get up to sharpen them. There may be many more such procedures, and over the years they may well run together for veteran students who forget from time to time which procedure *this* particular teacher prefers.

If each of seven teachers over two days of an A/B block schedule announce a different set of procedures for several identical classroom tasks (handing in homework, getting the students' attention, restroom policy), many, perhaps most, students are going to find it difficult to remember *which* teachers require *what*. The teacher who takes the time during the first week of school to practice these procedures over and over again will make them routine and reduce the chances that students will forget what needs to be done. One elementary teacher has her students practice cleaning up the classroom to one song and line up to another song until it is automatic. She plays one song and they clean up. She plays the other song and they line up. This teacher was once in the front row of one of my workshops, and when I played (unintentionally) her line-up song, *she stood and took a couple of steps before realizing she was a victim of her own (well established) routine.* It was a bit embarrassing, as she will admit today, but what happened to her is evidence that it works! Procedures must be practiced until they are routine.

Help students learn to share information with one another

The isolationist tendencies of teachers left to their own devices can spill over into the classroom, where students too often sit at their desks, doing seatwork and completing worksheets hour after hour. Goodlad (2004) and his team of researchers visited 1,000 classrooms in 38 schools and observed that rarely were students "actively engaged in learning directly from one another or in initiating processes of interaction with teachers" (p. 124). Sitting still for long periods does not provide the kind of stimulation the brain needs; simply standing up sends more blood to the brain, carrying with it oxygen and glucose for energy. Getting kids up and interacting with one another in conversation is a bonus, and working in pairs or groups to discuss something offers each team member a possibly different perspective. Students can also contribute opinions, stories, or examples, providing a richer context for learning. The brain is a connection-making organ, and seeing the same thing from different angles or points of view increases the number of neural connections, according to Jensen (2004), and he suggests maximizing "the number of connections they make by providing multiple contexts for learning the same thing" (p. 2).

Mentor/Protégé Focus

Through the use of reflective conversations on how kids (and adults!) learn best, mentors can help protégés surface insights and understandings related to the efficacy of classroom movement. New teachers may know sitting still for long periods of time is counterproductive, but if their recent instructional model in high school and college was lecture and seatwork, they may let students fall into that passive mode.

Having students stand with a partner (pair share) or in a trio or quartet (pairs squared) permits discussion, and teachers can move about among the pairs or groups listening to the conversations in order to gauge whether students understand or need a bit more direct instruction before moving on. Before having students tackle content in a paired discussion, teachers need to have them practice talking to each other about topics with which they are readily familiar: favorite foods, movies, music, vacations, or books. Once students have become used to sharing ideas, thoughts, and opinions with others (many others!), then the teacher can move on to topics related to subject-area content. That first week of school should be used to practice, practice, and practice again the art of talking and listening to other students, using familiar and nonthreatening topics of conversation before moving on to more difficult material.

Make clear what students can expect

Many teachers take the time to let students know exactly what they expect of them over the course of the school year, but how many lay out during the first week of school exactly what students can expect of them? Students can also be part of deciding what they can expect from the teacher. For example, I once had a conversation with my classes concerning the appropriate number of days before I returned quizzes and tests to them. They expressed frustration at having to wait weeks, in some classes, to get the results back, and we agreed that while a one-day return policy was a bit unrealistic, three days was about right. I agreed to that three-day policy and stuck with it for the rest of the year. On my year-end evaluations from the students, one of them remembered that conversation and indicated his appreciation at being part of the discussion and decision.

Teachers might spend some time talking with students about why remaining calm is a positive trait for teachers and students alike. Other expectations might include showing students a scoring rubric that they can count on to be used for the grading of essays. Teachers can even spend part of that first week having students practice with the rubric by having them grade sample essays. This will give them an appreciation of the time and effort it takes to grade essays, and it will give parents something to serve as a guide when helping students with those essays.

Certainty about most things is preferable to uncertainty, and this is true for teachers as well as students. A clear and understandable explanation of a teacher's homework policy would also be of interest to students, and it is an opportunity for the teacher to explain just what kinds of homework will be given, along with the forms feedback will take. If students understand that teachers will actually read assignments and provide constructive feedback, they are much more likely to turn it in at the appointed time. On the other hand, I once observed a teacher throw the homework in the trash can *the moment she received it!* It may not be necessary to explain the impact or long-term result of having done that.

Use music in the classroom

In *The Active Classroom* (2008), I devoted an entire chapter to the use of music as a process-facilitator in the classroom. As we have seen, some teachers use music as a cue to begin the clean-up process as well as to accompany the end-of-class lineup along the wall near the door. In each case, the only time the teachers use that particular piece of music is to cue those activities. One teacher told me her kids lined up when they were supposed to get their materials out near the beginning of class; she quickly realized she had played the wrong song, triggering that Pavlovian response. They simply did what the music told them to do.

We all know that there are kids who would rather die than be overheard by the entire class. One way to "hide" student-to-student conversations is by using music as a "cover" for conversations. With the music playing at a fairly loud level, students can feel free to talk and not be overheard by anyone except their face-to-face partners. Raising the volume quickly and hitting the pause button on the remote does a great job of bringing students back from their conversations. I once inadvertently hit the pause button while my workshop attendees were talking and the room immediately fell silent. It works because their minds register the fact that something has changed dramatically in the room—in this case the music to which they had gotten accustomed had stopped abruptly, causing them to get quiet and turn in my direction.

Music can also be used when students come into the room and when they leave it. Music energizes, and Allen (2010) reminds us that the lives of today's students are accompanied by "an almost permanent soundtrack," and "the only time it stops is in the classroom" (p. 116). I have been in scores of classrooms where music is a regular part of the auditory landscape, and appropriately used, it is a great motivator and process facilitator. Part of that first week of school can be used to introduce the uses of music and explain to students exactly why and when it will be used. Below is a list of some basic ways in which music can be used.

- As students enter the classroom
- As students get up and move into pairs, trios, or groups
- As a "cover" for student-to-student conversations
- As students go back to their seats after conversations
- As a cue for cleaning up the work area or desks
- As a cue to line up and get ready to go to the next class

Establish classroom norms

The first week of school is the time to establish rules and consequences and to discuss with the class what is acceptable and what is not in terms of behavior. Some teachers actually involve students in determining what the rules will be, making certain that they reserve the right to fill in any gaps. Whether the rules are presented or created from more-or-less whole cloth with considerable input from students, they must be clear, and I would also suggest they be few.

The fact that students need to raise their hands in order to receive permission to sharpen a pencil is not a rule; it is a procedure. Respecting others, according to Wong and Wong (2005), is a general rule that can encompass many specific examples (p. 145). Students may be involved in the creation or discussion of classroom rules; but rules at the school or district level are not open to changing at the classroom level, although they can be discussed (Wong & Wong, 2005). Allowing students some ownership of your classroom rules may help when it comes to enforcement. Mentors can work with protégés in differentiating between rules and procedures, with an eye toward keeping things clear, consistent, and simple.

Final Thoughts

That first week of school with students presents an opportunity for teachers to perfect the system that will carry everyone through the rest of the school year. Procedures can be practiced, practiced, and practiced some more. Expectations can be established and discussed. Rules can be decided upon or presented and explained to students, so what each rule means is clear. The first week is a great time to let students raise questions about all these things, so ambiguities can be clarified and week two can be devoted to shifting into second gear, *with processes in place that will guide instruction and behavior for the rest of the year.*

Mentors should take advantage of every opportunity to reflect with protégés on their own experiences as students in classrooms where teachers took the time to lay the foundation for a successful year during that first week. I'm just as certain that any such conversation will surface some recollections of classrooms where teachers jumped into course content so quickly that expectations went unstated, procedures went unlearned, and rules went unheeded. If mentors can get protégés to agree that spending that first week with students is critical for foundation building, those new teachers will have far fewer problems come November and December.

New teachers who do not frontload their school year with reflection, planning, and collaboration are more likely to experience problems because they will be forced to react to situations they have not considered and deal with obstacles they may not be prepared to overcome. It is the responsibility of the induction program to help novice teachers take the time to see how everything they do on a daily basis contributes to the big picture—teacher effectiveness and student progress over time.

In Chapter 6, we'll highlight the instructional focus that is critical to any induction program.

6

Everything in Its Place

U ltimately, any induction program for new teachers has to be about instruction. It isn't about orderly kids in orderly rows, and it isn't about making the trains run on time. It's about instruction. It's about Eddie being able to do something today he couldn't do yesterday, with the resultant satisfaction experienced by Eddie, his parents, and his teacher. It's about Eddie subsequently being confident he can do something else *tomorrow* he can't do *today*. It's about getting Eddie engaged in his own learning and shifting him from passive observer to active participant.

It's about Eddie, and it's about instruction.

Find and Ask the Right Questions

Later in the chapter, we'll take a look inside a classroom where students actively participate in their own learning while the teacher facilitates process. When new teachers—or any teachers—visit classrooms, they should be armed with a few questions that can be answered during the observation. Although the following list is long, the number of questions that accompany the observing teacher into the classroom should be short. The list below assumes that student interaction is a critical part of the learning process.

- Is the classroom arranged to allow for student movement and interaction?
- Are students given the opportunity to stand and move?

- If so, do they seem to appreciate the chance to do so?
- Does the teacher provide time for students to interact in pairs or groups?
- If so, do students seem to be comfortable working in pairs or groups?
- Do the students appear to be engaged in the content?
- Does the teacher allow at least three seconds of wait time after asking a question?
- Does the teacher appear to acknowledge various learning styles?
- Does this seem to be a safe environment where students are not afraid to share?
- Are directions for an activity clear? Is there a visual backup for auditory directions?
- Who seems to be doing most of the work, the students or the teacher?

Mentors can work with new teachers to develop a short list of questions prior to an observation. Rather than simply sitting and observing in another teacher's classroom, protégés can use four or five questions to provide focus during the time they are in the room. The above questions deal with process, and process is essential for a smooth-running classroom. Content is critical, obviously, but a teacher who knows her content but can't get a handle on process is going to find the going tough within a few short weeks. No matter when teachers are hired, mentors need to address instruction-related processes and strategies early on. One great way to begin is by letting protégés observe experienced teachers who understand the importance of a classroom organizational system composed of smoothly functioning processes. In this chapter we'll go inside a fictional classroom to see how the observation and the follow-up conference might go.

Hit the Ground Running

In Shellie's case, as we have seen, Mr. Crandall and Trey met with her immediately and arranged for her to see two superb teachers in action. They wanted her to see what could be accomplished when the focus is laser sharp and directly related to instruction and student progress. The reflective process began shortly after Shellie observed those classes, with Trey asking the kind of questions that would first cause her to think about and then attempt to understand what she had seen and heard in both classrooms; Trey then facilitated a discussion on application: *How could what she saw, heard, and understood be put to good use instructionally in her own social studies classroom?*

It is important to understand that what Trey did *not* do was to give her advice from his "many years of experience in these matters." Rather, he relied on Shellie's own observation, reflection, and understanding in order to arrive at some conclusions about the efficacy of instruction gleaned from the evidence of her own eyes and ears. Trey did not *tell* her what was effective, any more than he told her what she should do. Having observed two classrooms where instruction was the main focus, Shellie's mind was opened to the possibilities with Trey's skillful inquiry. Trey listened more than he talked, asked more questions than he answered, and Shellie did the rest. Down the road, there would be more opportunities for Shellie to observe other classes and talk with other teachers. The principal, Mr. Crandall, would have agreed with James Rowley (2005) that the opportunity for leadership is "the chance to help mentoring programs reach their fullest potential by assisting novice teachers in providing the best possible instruction for their students" (p. 123).

A Visit to Mrs. Bondurant's Classroom

In one of the classrooms Shellie visited, the first thing that struck her was the room arrangement (Figure 5.1 in Chapter 5), one that left a large open space in the middle of the room. The teacher, Mrs. Bondurant, began by referencing some formal writing her seventh graders had completed on the topic of abolitionism. The students had picked up their rough-draft essays on the way into the classroom, and Mrs. Bondurant gave them a few moments to look over the written feedback she had provided. After instructing them to complete their final abolitionist essay drafts outside of class, she had her students put the essays into their folders, which Shellie noticed had a closed top that was fastened by a small metal snap. Mrs. Bondurant aimed a small remote at the MP3 player/sound system on her desk, and the sound of an upbeat song accompanied this small bit of housekeeping.

When the essays had been put away, Mrs. Bondurant stood on a small step stool in the front of the room, remote in hand, and said, "Stand up!" As she said this she brought her arms up in a sweeping gesture, and soon all her seventh graders were standing behind their chairs, and the chairs had been pushed under their desks. Then she issued another command, saying, "In a moment, when I say go, find a partner other than someone at your quad, with whom you have not met this week . . . Go!" Behind her back, she must have hit the play button on the remote, because Dion's *The Wanderer* began to play as the students paired off in the large open area in the center of the room, right in front of Mrs. Bondurant. She raised the volume of the music and cut it off abruptly, saying, "Look this way please!" In their pairs, they got quiet and turned toward her. Shellie thought, *They've done this before.*

From the stool, Mrs. Bondurant said, "Decide who will be A and who will be B!" Then, "If you are A, raise your hand. Hands down. If you are B, raise your hand. Okay, hands down." She paused for a moment, and then said, "PVF!"

Shellie thought, *What is PVF?* The kids did not seem to be confused, however, and Mrs. Bondurant introduced the activity: "If you are an A, when I say go you will begin the conversation. If you are B, you will adopt your supportive stance and listen carefully to A as he or she talks. After about a minute, when I say 'switch' and stop the music, B will take over and summarize what A said."

Mrs. Bondurant looked around the room, and seeing no confusion on their faces, continued, "The topic of conversation is the topic of your essays—abolitionism. Yesterday, we saw a short video clip and discussed the effect of the abolitionist activities on border towns in southern Ohio and in communities in northern North Carolina. Your job if you are an A is to describe how abolitionism affected life in the border communities above and below the Mason-Dixon Line."

Mrs. Bondurant gave everyone a moment, and then she said, "Face your partner. When I say go, A will start the conversation. When I say 'switch' B will summarize. Ready, go!" As she said that, she started some music using her remote and the kids went to work. Mrs. Bondurant came down from the step stool and began to circulate around the periphery of the crowd of students in the center of the room. After a minute or so, she raised volume of the music and cut it off, saying, "Okay, finish your thought and switch!" As Shellie watched from her chair by the closet, those designated as B started summarizing what their A partners had said. Shellie had never seen anything like this, and she made a note to ask Mrs. Bondurant about the strategy after class.

After maybe 30 seconds, Mrs. Bondurant, up on the stool again, raised the volume and cut it off. The students stopped and thanked their partners; once again Shellie thought: *They've done this before, too.* From her vantage point on the step stool, Mrs. Bondurant must have hit the play button again, because once again *The Wanderer* accompanied the students to their seats. Finally, Mrs. Bondurant had them say "welcome back" to their quad partners, at which point she increased the volume and cut the music off, and the kids turned to face her.

Shellie was amazed, and maybe a little awestruck. She had indeed been watching these seventh graders, and their body language told her they had enjoyed the entire activity. They had moved, paired, shared, thanked each other, and landed back in their seats with no fuss or confusion. They had obviously become used to doing this, and she circled the PVF notation she had made in her notebook, making a further mental note to ask Mrs. Bondurant about it. At the end of the class period, as the students left the room to yet another upbeat song, Shellie gathered her purse and notebook. She waited until the kids were gone to approach Mrs. Bondurant, whose preparation period followed this one.

The two of them sat down at one of the quads, and Shellie placed her notes in front of her. They made small talk for a few minutes, and discovered they had both graduated from the same university only four years apart. Mrs. Bondurant, or Katie, as she now encouraged Shellie to call her, had been lucky enough to land at a school that valued its new teachers and their development as much as the leadership team at Shellie's new school. Katie had been able to visit several outstanding classrooms during the course of *her* first three years, and admitted she had her eyes opened.

"Honestly," said Katie, "Had there been no induction program here, the classroom you saw today might not have developed along these lines. Because they worked with me early—and I had a wonderful mentor by the way—I avoided the isolationist tendencies I see at other schools where collaboration and support are simply not available."

"I can't remember seeing a classroom where the students were so engaged," said Shellie. "They seem to thrive in here, and I did not see one discipline issue for the entire class period."

Katie smiled. "I appreciate the compliment. Actually, I have not written a discipline referral in four years. I attribute that to the fact that I don't contribute to what I consider 'pressure-cooker' teaching by making the kids sit all period long, watching video after video, doing worksheets, or listening to me babble on about this or that. I learned early, thank goodness, that the kids need to be doing the work. My job in here, as you saw, is to facilitate process. In other words, I *model* and they *do*. I *model* and they *do*. They need to be engaged in their own learning."

Shellie looked at her notes, saying, "What is PVF?"

Katie laughed. "After months of using that strategy I have stopped spelling it out. PVF stands for Paired Verbal Fluency, and I first saw it used in a workshop during my first year of teaching. The idea is that if two students are asked to share, one of them may dominate the conversation to the detriment of the other. PVF provides a structure where each partner gets to talk while the other listens. The listener then summarizes what his partner said. My job as a facilitator of that process is to time it and to listen in on some of the conversations. I'll give you a copy of the directions" (Figure 6.1).

Figure 6.1   Paired Verbal Fluency

PVF as a step-by-step activity, with directions

Note: Give the directions one at a time.

Direction: "Stand up, and find a partner other than someone at your table."

Direction: "Decide who will be **A** and who will be **B**."

Direction: "**A**, raise your hand; and **B**, raise your hand." Then, "Hands down!"

Direction: "Our topic for discussion is _____. **A**, when I say, 'Go!' I'll give you 60 seconds to talk about the topic. Now **B**, while **A** is talking, listen carefully. When I say, 'Switch!' **B** will summarize what **A** said. In order to be able to do that effectively, you must listen carefully while **A** is speaking."

Direction: "Look at the board once again to see the topic."

Direction: "**A**, you're on . . . Go!"

Partner **A** speaks directly to Partner **B** for 60 seconds on the chosen topic.

Direction: After 60 seconds, the teacher says, "Switch!"

Partner **B** summarizes what **A** said.

Direction: After 30 seconds, the teacher says, "Stop! Look this way."

Direction: "Well done. Thank your partner for sharing. On to the next step."

Direction: "This time, **B** will go first. As you think about the two-minute conversation you and **A** had a few moments ago, were there some things left undiscussed, something important left out? When I say 'Go!' you'll have 60 seconds to add whatever you think has yet to be discussed as it relates to the topic. When I say 'Switch!' **A** will have 30 seconds to summarize what you said."

Direction: "**B**, you're on . . . Go!"

On the same topic, Partner **B** goes first and adds whatever he thinks might have been left out of the initial conversation.

Direction: After 60 seconds, the teacher says, "Switch!"

Partner **A** summarizes what **B** said.

Direction: After 30 seconds, the teacher says, "Pause . . . and look this way!"

Direction: "Thank your partner, give each other a gentle high five, and take your seats!"

Shellie said, "Why listen in to the conversations?"

Katie thought for a moment. "Well, for three reasons, I guess. First, I want to make sure they are on task, and circulating and listening sends the message that I *want to know* if they are on task. Second, by listening to the conversations, I can see if they seem to understand the topic under discussion. Finally, if I overhear some great conversation—especially on the part of someone who for the first time really 'gets it'—I can ask that student if he or she is willing to share with the whole class. If they say yes, then I invite them to share later on, after the activity is over. If they say no, they would rather not share right now, I say, 'That's okay, maybe later,' and I move on. These structured conversations are great ways for them to process information and sort of tie it all together. Not only do they learn to explain something they also learn to summarize, and that skill is an important part of comprehension. Knowing they are going to have to summarize makes them listen more carefully. They also learn from each other."

Shellie said, "I noticed that once they were seated, you asked how many had learned something from their partner. Most of them raised their hands."

Katie smiled. "I did that for your benefit, I guess, although I often ask that question, and I get the same results. Kids can learn from each other, and they are often more effective at making their friends understand something than I."

"It occurred to me more than once, Katie, that your students had everything down pat, and I also noticed that their body language was controlled. Those who were doing the listening had their hands at their sides and did not seem to be distracting."

"During the first week of school," Katie explained, "I did nothing but establish and practice all these things. They practiced standing and pushing their chairs under their desks. They all practiced the supportive stance you noticed (Figure 6.2). They worked over and over again on explaining, summarizing, giving examples to clarify an explanation, and thanking each other before sitting down. We worked on all sorts of basic procedures, and we arrived at a basic set of ground rules to support a safe climate. You may have noticed that no one in here refused to share, and that is a result of having spent much of the first week discussing how we could make this an environment where everyone can take risks without being razzed or laughed at by classmates."

Shellie wanted to give Katie Bondurant some time to herself before the students arrived for the next class period, so she thanked her, paying her several compliments and congratulating her on the

Figure 6.2   Kid Listening, With Hands Down

Created by Brian T. Jones

way in which she got her students to engage at several levels of the cognitive ladder—from general knowledge to explanation to summarization. On the way out of the building, she began to compare what she had just seen with most of her experiences in middle and high school. What she was used to as part of her experience stood in stark contrast to Katie's class, and she spent the rest of the drive home reflecting on what she had seen.

As has already been mentioned, early on in any induction program—and before the end of the school year if teachers are hired in the spring with a start date in the fall—opportunities should be provided for new teachers to observe the classrooms of teachers who display the qualities we explored in Chapter 1. At the same time we introduce them to subject-area standards, we should let them know that there are standards of instructional practice as well. During the first two years of the induction program, observations should be regularly scheduled, and workshops should be provided where teachers (new or veteran) can pick up new ideas and reflect on the state of the art in as it pertains to instruction.

Shifting the Work Load to the Students

I have seen teachers who work hard without getting results because it is they—and not their students—who are doing the lion's share of the work. Great teachers work incredibly hard, but they make certain that their students are working harder, working smarter, and developing their thinking skills in a way that will benefit them not only in school but also in life outside the schoolhouse.

As teachers facilitate student progress, the kids need to see a teacher who loves what he or she does. Great teachers have an underlying passion that drives them. "It is this passion," says Jackson (2009), "that will help you stay the course in spite of overwhelming constraints even when it feels easier or saner to just give up" (p. 204). Students who see that passion at work every day are, I believe, much more likely to accept what they must do to succeed; they are much more likely to willingly engage themselves in their own learning. I recently heard the story of a student who was asked if he wanted to be a teacher. "Are you kidding? Why would I want to be that miserable?" That particular story and quote may or may not be true, but I have heard that sentiment on the part of students over the years. I have seen teachers who are truly miserable, dragging their students kicking and screaming through an entire school year.

New teachers must make classroom visits to teachers who love what they are doing and are good at it. A protégé must see a mentor who not only loves teaching, but who truly enjoys working with new teachers. In the same way that great teachers inspire students, mentors must work to inspire their protégés and lead by example. Imagine a mentor who sits down with his protégé on the first day of inservice week in August, then

> ### Mentor/Protégé Focus
>
> When mentors work with administrators to arrange protégé visits to other classrooms, the teachers they choose for observation should be those who love what they are doing, as well as understand the importance of engaging students in their own learning.

sighs and says, "Well, let's get this checklist done so you can get back to your classroom." Anything close to this sets the wrong tone, and the comment may well lead the new teacher to speculate that this is how the mentor starts his classes—and this may well be the case.

Teaching involves perspiration and inspiration in perhaps equal parts, but the really heavy lifting needs to be done by students engaged in their own learning. Induction programs need to lead by example;

building administrators need to get the faculty engaged just as deeply and effectively in their own continuous-improvement process. Administrators in successful systems model effective instruction by turning faculty meetings that may once have been information dumps into truly reflective and collaborative experiences. New teachers who are part of an overall school- and/or district-based continuous-improvement model will benefit tremendously, as will their students.

From Providing Information to Facilitating the Learning Process

The whole idea of giving people information and leaving the rest up to them may not be successful in a mentor-protégé relationship any more than giving students information and leaving the rest up to them is successful as part of a teacher-student relationship. Teachers at any level who believe their sole function is to provide information are missing the mark. In an age where humans are inundated with information from every direction and at every hour of the day and night, the job of teachers is to help students sort through and *make meaning* of the information. To illustrate this, let's go back for a moment to the end of the industrial age in America, just prior to the advent of personal computers that dragged many of us kicking and screaming into the information age.

In the late 1970s, I was several years into my teaching career. Just into the winter break one year, our high school library was gutted by fire. Much of that holiday week was subsequently spent in cleaning the rest of the building, heavily damaged by smoke and water. The cleaning was thorough, although the smell remained, and school resumed on time after the holidays; but our entire collection of books, periodicals, and reference materials had disappeared overnight. There were, of course, no backup discs, no flash drives, and no net-work storage capabilities. The print media on which we relied for term-paper research, book reports, or to answer simple questions on any number of topics went up in flames; it took years to recover from the loss.

As social studies department chair, part of my job that winter and spring was to assist the librarian in ordering new materials in my subject area. I ordered the newest edition of the Dictionary of American Biography and the Dictionary of National Biography (British), along with hundreds of other titles related to geography, history, economics, and political science. In the late 1970s, our only option was to replace print resources with print resources that were out of date the moment they went to press. We thought nothing of that, and while we lamented the loss of so much we did rejoice in being able to replenish using insurance money.

For months we rebuilt, ordered new books, and referred students to the town library for their research needs. Well into the process, one of our teachers asked me for information about Benjamin Franklin. His daughter was writing a paper on Franklin, and as a history teacher I was a natural source of information on the topic. I suggested, as I recall, two biographies; I also suggested he call the librarian at the town library to see if she had the Dictionary of American Biography in the stacks. Talking to me had thus given that teacher three "hits" in the course of a conversation that lasted maybe two minutes. A few minutes ago, while typing this manuscript, I Googled Benjamin Franklin—limiting the number of potential hits with qualifiers—and received 4,700,000 hits in the course of maybe two seconds. Times have changed. Getting information is simply not a problem in the 21st century; and today, that teacher who asked me about Ben Franklin would not even bother coming to me. He would choose his search engine of choice and click away.

The role of teachers as "purveyors of information" has been diminished by the availability of electronic resources unimaginable in the 1970s. Teachers today can't possibly compete with information sources available to students electronically; the role of teachers today is to help students ponder, grapple with, and make sense of what they see and hear in an age where limitless information comes at them with ever-increasing volume and speed. Relieved of the need to be the sole source of information, teachers today increasingly need to be able to help students compare, contrast, infer, evaluate, explain, defend, and otherwise think critically in the face of vast amounts of largely unfiltered and often-misleading data.

> ### Mentor/Protégé Focus
>
> One of the best reflective conversations a mentor can have with a protégé concerns the role of the teacher vis-à-vis the vast amount of information available to students and teachers today. Mentors can help protégés explore the role of the teacher in helping students sift through and make sense of the information to which they have access at the click of a mouse.

A teacher who needs to teach her students to think critically and communicate effectively needs a mentor who can model these skills. Superficial, throwaway phrases like "call me if you need me" or "hang in there" are no longer, if indeed they ever were, of any real use to new teachers who find themselves unable to cope and ill-equipped to understand what their job really entails. Coming to the conclusion that they are incompetent and without real support, new teachers may begin to seek gainful employment elsewhere.

Teachers as Reflective Practitioners

Mentors, as role models for their protégés, would do well to constantly look at *how* they do *what* they do. Great teachers continually look for ways to become even better instructors. Those teachers who take the time to reflect frequently on what they see and do in their own and other classrooms set up their students and themselves for success. According to Bartell (2005), "Reflective teachers learn in and from their practice" (p. 138). They also learn from others, and they read journal articles and books related to the practice of teaching. In addition, a protégé who sees her mentor walking the talk is much more likely to follow suit and move in the direction of a reflective practitioner.

Induction programs that are part of an overall reflective atmosphere replete with collaborative inquiry and time set aside for deep reflection are much more likely to succeed. Mentors and protégés who seek to be reflective practitioners need "colleagues that share this perspective and will work with one another to improve practice for all teachers and more important, learning for all students" (Bartell, 2005, p. 138). Individual mentors and protégés trying to become reflective practitioners in an isolationist culture are going to find the going difficult. Administrators need to cultivate the kind of collaborative and reflective climate that will support the best efforts of mentors doing their level best to facilitate the growth of new teachers.

Final Thoughts

Instruction, then, must be a key focus of any mentor's work with a protégé. Jonson (2002) points out that "Teachers spend an overwhelming amount of time talking to students and socializing with each other but little time solving instructional problems together" (p. 38).

Mentors, even in a school culture where little professional dialogue takes place on a daily basis, need to make certain that their work with protégés includes plenty of time for reflective dialogue centering on instruction. If other mentors, protégés, and teachers can be brought into the discussions, so much the better.

In Chapter 7, we'll continue this line of thought by taking a close look at the whole idea of continuous improvement, with an eye toward making new teachers self-sufficient in the relentless pursuit of excellence.

7

When Good Gets Better

Continuous improvement is a journey without a finish line. For individual teachers, this is to say that no matter how good a teacher gets, it is always possible to get better. Organizationally, continuous improvement is an ongoing process by which every segment of the organization shares a set of beliefs and a vision, sets goals and benchmarks, analyzes results data that tells everyone where they are in the process, and willingly takes part in a reflective self-examination—all with the stated purpose of improving performance. Critical to this process is vision. To Schlechty (2001), leaders need to articulate the vision, that is, "what the world would look like if it were organized in ways that were consistent with one's beliefs," and they need to "inspire others to act in terms of the vision" (p. 193). The supervisor I spoke of in Chapter 4, articulated his vision in such a way that they became *our* beliefs and *our* vision.

The best situation for a new teacher would be to find herself in a school where the commitment to progress for each administrator, teacher, student, and staff member is interwoven into the fabric of the school community in one forward-looking effort at continuous improvement. An induction program that is developed as a part of a culture that already has, in the words of W. Edwards Deming, as quoted in Lezotte (1992), a "constancy of purpose toward improvement" (p. 6) may be more likely to succeed than in a school where improvement is at best a hit-and-miss effort. A school environment that is dedicated to measurable, relentless progress will best sustain an induction program that has as its basic tenet that same mantra of improvement for new teachers. A mentor who is part of this culture will have the advantage of having the support of administrators and colleagues completely familiar with goal setting, benchmarking, data analysis, and results.

Schools all over the country find themselves somewhere along a continuum from a consistent, highly effective approach to systemic improvement to those that improve, if at all, in fits and starts, with no common set of beliefs or articulated vision. In many schools, according to Zmuda and colleagues (2004), "teachers have replaced the collective continuous improvement model with a minimalist structure that endorses the autonomy of teachers to pursue their own best practices in lieu of reaching consensus" (p. 9). In those schools, improvement is in the hands of individual teachers or groups of teachers who make the effort because they see its advantages in terms of outcome. Getting better as a teacher translates into improvement on the part of students, and that commitment to progress should be part and parcel of any induction and mentoring program.

If teacher mentors have the luxury of operating within a school district and/or school-level organization dedicated to systemic improvement, so much the better. It may be that mentors have the support of their building administrators and otherwise are on their own to do what they think will be effective in support of a new teacher. In any case, it is critical that mentors not just be dispensers of advice or "those to whom new teachers go for answers." Regardless of the level of commitment to continuous improvement on the part of district- or school-level administrators, mentors should constantly be aware of the fact that the official relationship with their protégés will end at some point down the road, and those new teachers with whom they have worked will be best served if they possess tools that will allow them to operate inside their own continuous-improvement model.

Taking the Proverbial Bull by the Horns

Individual teachers can certainly operate under their own improvement model, regardless of the commitment from building administrators. Beginning with what they want students to accomplish, teachers can develop a set of beliefs and a vision of what students ought to be able to accomplish over a given period of time. Mentors can help accelerate this process by demonstrating for new teachers how they can check for understanding along the way with different formative assessment techniques that demonstrate where students are on their own pathways to progress. As we saw in Chapter 5, planning is critical, and mentors can work with new teachers early on to develop habits that will facilitate progress.

In a school where teacher isolationism is the norm, it is particularly important that a new teacher develop the ability to self-reflect and self-assess in order to make necessary adjustments or course changes in his or her continuous-improvement journey. New teachers who are *not* part of a school environment where continuous improvement is already an integral part of the landscape will benefit—as will their students—from a self-generated system of professional improvement that guarantees ongoing growth and development. Mentors can step in and fill this gap, if one exists, by working with new teachers to develop a plan for self-improvement that will serve their protégés well for the remainder of their careers.

In a school where professional development is left up to the individual teachers or small groups of teachers, the impact on those teachers' students can be significant; the impact on the school community as a whole may be minimal. In fact, Zmuda and others (2004) define the limits of any single teacher's own self-improvement model: "Staff members must confront the inescapable truth that their self-improvement model for professional growth will never achieve desired results in improved student achievement throughout the school" (p. 10). This is not to say that teachers should not pursue their own attempts at self-improvement, but the school as a whole will not move appreciably forward unless there is a collective commitment to growth and development that encompasses the entire staff. *Individual teachers, including mentors and protégés, don't need to wait for some major transformation at the school level before making a significant commitment to their own continuous improvement.*

In a workshop several years ago, another trainer and I had just gone over the basic components of a dynamic customer-service program when one of the participants raised her hand and said, "I wish the principal would adopt this program in our school!" We pointed out that while that would indeed be desirable, the fact that such a program has not been officially instituted does not mean that individuals or groups of individuals in the schoolhouse cannot or should not exemplify the core tenets of this or indeed any powerful customer-service philosophy. It is true that a collective—rather than an individual—approach to customer service in an organization is likely to have a greater impact for the entire organization in the long run.

Nevertheless, individual members of an organization committed to improving customer service can provide anecdotal evidence through their own efforts that change for the whole organization might just be something worth pursuing. Often, employees with a proven track record for excellent customer-service skills will seek employment in a company that as a whole reflects their own ideas of effective service and continuous improvement. I have seen schools begin to change as a result of the grassroots efforts of a few dynamic teachers dedicated to experimentation, innovation, and relentless progress.

Teachers as a Catalyst for Change

Teachers who experiment, innovate, self-reflect, and constantly improve student performance can serve as a catalyst for change in the building. For example, a relatively small group of teachers intent on continual progress can work to convince administrators to transform faculty meetings that are often information dumps into workshops dedicated to working on a core set of beliefs, discussing and arriving at a common vision, and eventually beginning the process of looking at schoolwide data in an attempt to spot areas of strength and weakness in the areas of curriculum and instructional delivery. Mentors, along with teachers in their formative years in the classroom, can serve as proponents of change as they serve as role models for their protégés and others within the building.

Improvement is a fluid and sometimes-messy process; it is messy because it involves an open and honest look at how we do what we do in the classroom and in the schoolhouse. When we look in the mirror, we may not like what we see; and if we take part in a reflective process of individual or organizational improvement, what we see may make us feel uncomfortable. A favorite 30-minute lecture that it appears is not connecting with students, or that does not result in appreciable growth for those students, may have to be discarded or adjusted so that students are given the opportunity to process the information in some way at the end of a 10-minute lecture on the same topic. The trick is to get new teachers to be self-reflective and self-evaluative to the extent that they can spot the weaknesses in the pedagogy surrounding the delivery of that material in the classroom.

A middle school teacher I knew years ago used to frequently ask her students how she was doing. They would anonymously post sticky notes on a chart with comments about the delivery of that particular lesson. She did this all day long in each of her classes; then she collected the notes and began to look for patterns. If several students from her four classes commented on the length of the lecture, she knew she might have to shorten her direct instruction next time in favor of more direct engagement on their part. She asked students to comment on what she was doing well; and she asked them to let her know where she might improve. Over the weeks and months, she was thus able to collect lots of valuable feedback she could use in her own continuous-improvement journey.

Mentors who work with protégés to facilitate the kind of reflective processing we spoke of earlier will do them a great service. If both the mentor and the protégé, after observing a lesson, think out loud about what they saw and heard, they are off and running toward identifying the import of what they observed. From making sense of what they saw, both can then explore the application possibilities. These reflective conversations will benefit not only the protégé, but the mentor as well, along with students in *both* classes. The moment this kind of collaborative processing becomes routine, the mentor has given her protégé a valuable tool for self-improvement. A new teacher who gets into the habit of looking deep inside *how* she does *what* she does is likely to be a lifelong learner who improves with each year in the profession.

> ### Mentor/Protégé Focus
>
> Mentors who assist new teachers in the development of a continuous improvement model based on self evaluation are doing their protégés a tremendous service. Teachers who can learn to take a look at how they do what they do on a regular basis are far more likely to succeed in the long run.

A Structure for Improvement

I enjoy watching great coaches at work, but what I generally observe when I look at coaches on the basketball court or in the dugout is but the tip of an extensive continuous improvement iceberg. Great coaches, like great teachers, always know exactly where they want to go. The vision is shared with the team; and on the improvement journey coaches observe players and provide feedback during practice sessions. Having made some adjustments, they do it again—once more studying the results and providing feedback. After looking at tapes and conferring with assistants, the process of practicing—observing—providing feedback—making adjustments—practicing—providing feedback—proceeds in a continuous cycle with performance improvement as the goal.

Conzemius and O'Neill (2002) illustrate this through the use of a PDSA (plan-do-study-act) cycle that is both simple and effective:

Plan a change or action;

Do the change or action (on a small scale at first);

Study the results to learn what did and did not work; and

Act by refining the idea or by implementing it on a broader scale. (p. 3)

Figure 7.1 demonstrates how a continuous improvement loop spirals off, always moving toward perfection (never arriving, of course).

Figure 7.1   Continuous Improvement Cycle (PDSA)

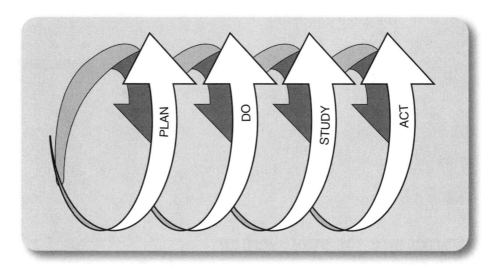

Created by Dianne Kinnison

PDSA Example

Shellie, in her first-period social studies class, has spent about 25 minutes covering the Underground Railroad as it operated in the 1850s United States. Specifically, she has been talking about the various routes north, the difficulties involved in getting to freedom after the Fugitive Slave Act was passed. For homework, her students had already read a short piece on Harriet Tubman and other conductors operating as part of a system that was pretty well established by the mid 1850s. She had read the first part of the story to them in class the day before, and had asked them to finish it that evening. Shellie would like to move onto another related topic, but she would like to be certain the kids are ready to do that. She knew from her own experience as a student and as a student teacher that if she simply asked the kids if anyone understood, they would all nod their heads and no one would be willing to say he or she was the one kid in the class who didn't get it. The questions, *Does everyone understand?* and *Does anyone have questions?* were both pretty much dead ends, and they would tell her nothing. She had learned that her students were unwilling to share with their peers that they did not understand, even if it was true.

In one of the district-sponsored workshops she had attended in early fall, Shellie had learned about a quick check-for-understanding piece called the traffic light technique. Her students had at their desks small envelopes with three small cards. On each card was the outline of a traffic light; one of the cards had the green light colored in, and each of the other two had either a yellow light or red light. They had done this many times in class since the workshop; all the kids had to do was palm one of the three cards with the traffic light turned toward her: The student who showed her the card with the green light was saying he or she understood the concept or topic well enough to teach it to someone else. Turning the yellow light toward Shellie indicated that a few more examples might help; showing her a red light meant a lack of understanding on the part of her students.

Shellie had found that if, once all the cards were palmed and turned her way, she was looking at a sea of green she could move on. A few green lights mixed in with a good many yellow lights meant she probably needed to give them a few more examples, or simply spend a bit more time on the concept or topic. Many red lights indicated to Shellie that she needed to approach the subject from a different angle or teach it in a different way, for the simple reason that many or most kids simply did not understand. The kids had learned how to palm the cards so no one but Shellie could see them. This made the whole self-assessment process both private and valuable.

In the case of the last half hour spent on the Underground Railroad, Shellie saw mostly green lights with a few yellow lights and one red light. She decided to put the kids in trios or quartets and have them discuss with each other what they had learned concerning this topic while it was still relatively fresh in their minds. She had learned that sometimes kids can teach things to each other in a way that is far more effective, so she had the kids stand and move into trios or groups no larger than four. Once they were grouped, she asked them to discuss with each other what they knew about the Underground Railroad while she circulated among the groups. What she heard as she passed from group to group told her they had a pretty good grasp of the topic.

Shellie had them thank their partners for sharing, and once they were seated she brought up two or three more points in order to clear up some misunderstandings she overheard as she circulated during the activity. She then had them hold up their traffic light cards again and with satisfaction noticed a sea of green, along with one yellow light. She made a mental note to talk to that student later on, and then played a piece of music that was the signal for the students to get their desks cleaned and straightened before moving to the next class period. Having the students discuss the Underground Railroad had cost an extra fifteen minutes, but it also provided the students with an opportunity to process what they had learned, and by so doing ensure that more of them understood and remembered what they had covered during the class period.

It was Trey, her mentor, who had taught her the PDSA cycle as an improvement tool. Over the course of several months, Shellie had become used to planning something, following the plan, assessing it in some formative manner, and then making adjustments. Trey, in his observations of Shellie's classes, knew that this habit would serve her and her students well over the course of her career.

Teachers, like coaches, need to first arrive at a goal and then determine what actions will move students along this improvement spiral toward that goal. Teachers model and then have the kids do, at which point teachers will observe, assess, and provide feedback that makes adjustment possible. My experience is that many teachers get caught up in the do cycle, and so it becomes circular, as in Figure 7.2. In order to make continuous progress toward the vision, something has to change each time. Otherwise, the loop will become closed as the students simply mark time without any clear and useful feedback that would allow for improvement—and, eventually, significant progress.

Figure 7.2   Do Cycle (Closed Loop)

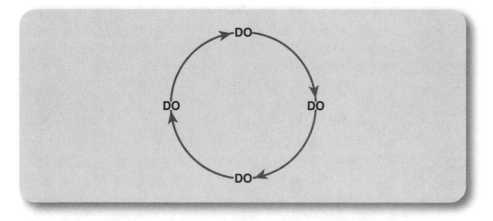

Created by Dianne Kinnison

Checking for Understanding

Mentors can work with protégés to provide frequent opportunities to assess student progress through the use of formative assessments. Summative assessments, especially final exams and those ubiquitous state tests, provide teachers with feedback for the improvement of instruction from one year to the next. Summative tests do not, however, by their very "final" nature, help students in their continuous-improvement journeys because those tests "are designed to provide feedback on how the student performed after instruction" (Fisher & Frey, 2007). Formative assessments, as defined by Burke (2005), "are used to monitor students' progress and provide immediate and meaningful feedback as to what students have to do to achieve learning standards" (p. xx). As students seek to make progress on a daily basis, then, formative assessments are designed to let students know how far they have moved toward a clearly defined goal. These assessments are not given for the purpose of providing a grade; their purpose is to check for understanding and provide feedback in order that necessary adjustments or course corrections can be made.

> **Mentor/Protégé Focus**
>
> One great reflective conversation among mentors and protégés in the building could concern the importance of frequent checks for understanding in the classroom. One way to do this would be to have everyone in the group read the same one or two articles on formative assessment, followed by a discussion of key points and strategies.

An example of something that can serve as a powerful formative assessment tool is the student portfolio, a working definition of which was developed by the Northwest Regional Educational Laboratory in Portland, Oregon, and can be found in Burke (2005): "A portfolio is a collection of student work gathered for a particular purpose that exhibits to the student and others the student's efforts, progress or achievement in one or more areas" (p. 56).

A student portfolio is not simply a collection of "stuff" students accumulate over time in a binder or folder. It is, as the definition above makes clear, gathered for a particular purpose. It might, for example, demonstrate the development in a student's progress in writing over a period of time. According to Burke (2005), it can be used to

1. Document meeting district, state, or national standards;

2. Connect several subject areas to provide an integrated assessment of the student;

3. Chronicle a student's growth and development over extended periods of a semester, year, or clusters of grades (K–2, 3–5, 7–9, 10–12, etc.);

4. Document the key concepts taught by teachers; and

5. Share at a job interview, promotion, or college entrance review. (p. 57)

Several years ago, I visited an extraordinary high school science classroom. A student met me at the door; everyone, including the teacher, was either standing or seated on stools around various large black tables. The student who initially welcomed me went on to show me various run charts on the walls, each of them indicating collective progress on various types of assessments. He explained this was so that the class could see exactly how they were moving forward (or not) in their continuous-improvement journey. Next, he showed me his personal portfolio. He had his own run charts showing personal progress over time, and the binder contained written work of various sorts that contained tons of feedback from the teacher. In speaking with various members of the class (juniors) near the end of the period, they all spoke the language of continuous improvement.

They mentioned several things related to the collective growth of the class, including the fact that when assessment results were posted on the wall each week, the teacher facilitated a reflective conversation on why they went up or down as a class. They actually analyzed the results and brainstormed possible variables (the "big game" on the night before the test, lack of sufficient review, not enough class time spent on the concepts, and so on) that might have led to a marked falling off of scores. Here was the best part for me as an observer: The teacher did not accept anything less than an A grade from anyone. The students kept track of everything in the portfolios, they worked with each other to improve based on the teacher's frequent feedback as reflected in the written pieces, and they shared in a common vision and a belief that they could—given enough time and assistance—bring the grades up.

The portfolios I saw as I walked around the room talking with students showed constant progress, and they could not wait to show the binders to me. Furthermore, they loved that class. They laughed when they told me about their other classes, where they continually fell asleep or stared out the windows daydreaming or otherwise mentally disconnected from the constant lecturing and teacher talk. In this science class, they were engaged, reflective, organized participants in their own learning. They knew where they were going, and they helped each other get there in as good an example of collective accountability as I have seen in almost 40 years in education. The science teacher facilitated their progress by providing constant feedback, leading them in reflective conversations, and helping them create a system of self-assessment that was both systemic and ultimately effective.

That classroom visit was in the early 1990s. Today's portfolios would, in many cases, be electronic rather than paper. Items for a student's portfolio can be collected throughout the year, and at the end of the year—and in the face of what might be a daunting amount of student work—teachers and students can decide what goes into the final portfolio. For students working with their portfolios, self-reflection is every bit as critical as it is for protégés as they work with mentors. Students can reflect on what in their body of work they consider to be their best work, their most difficult, or most creative (Burke, 2005, p. 65). These reflections can be added to their portfolios, providing valuable insight during their continuous-improvement journey. Portfolios also provide parents with a window into what their kids are accomplishing in school. Parents can see firsthand what progress has been made.

Silence Is Golden (and Useful)

Making sure students understand can sometimes be a function of providing periods of silence, allowing students to process information. When observing classrooms around the country, I make it a point to watch the students, not the teachers. Teachers often do not provide enough periods of silence (wait time) to permit kids to think and process what they have just heard or seen. Walsh and Sattes (2005), after looking at existing research on this topic, report that when teachers ask a question or receive an answer from students, the *result* of waiting three to five seconds before responding is that "more students participate in class discussion, their answers are longer and of a higher quality, and achievement improves on cognitively complex measures" (p. 14). Teachers who respond immediately do not give students a chance to process.

This is true of adults as well, and in many a college classroom I have sometimes felt like I was trying to sip from a fire hose; in those cases information was coming at me so quickly I was unable to process what my brain wanted to process because the next point or topic was already on the way from the professor. Novice teachers fresh out of a teacher preparation program may have experienced rapid-fire lectures that did not provide time for immediate processing. In years of working with mentors, new teachers, and recent college graduates who are substitute teaching until they can obtain a full-time teaching job, this always comes up in discussions about instructional-delivery methodology. If the questioning techniques of professors did not include sufficient wait time then mentors can surface this reality in reflective conversations with protégés. Mentors can model the use of silence as a cognitive tool by slowing down the pace of conversations between themselves and protégés; mentors can discuss with these new teachers the applications for their own classrooms.

Suggestions for Mentors

What follows is a series of suggestions for teacher mentors related to working with protégés on continuous improvement. As I mentioned earlier in this chapter, it is critical that mentors not become the "answer person" for protégés in areas in which it is critical for new teachers to develop their own capacity for solving problems, removing obstacles, and improving continuously in a way that is both systemic and relentless. We have seen that even in an isolationist school culture where professional development and process improvement is left up to individuals and small groups, mentors can work with protégés to build a self-reflective and self-assessing capacity.

Bigger Groups and More Perspectives

Bring together all the mentors and protégés in the school as early as possible to talk about critical issues such as continuous improvement. Four mentors and four new teachers, for example, provide eight different perspectives in looking at multiple issues; my experience is that the larger groups also provide more energy. Involving everyone provides a richer context that comes from the collective experiences of the larger group. One mentor can facilitate the conversation, and someone else from the group can capture ideas on chart paper. The plan-do-study-act cycle could be introduced at one point, and ways of implementing that in the classroom could be surfaced for general discussion and comment. What might come out of one or a series of conversations is a plan for implementing a system of continuous improvement in the classrooms of all eight teachers, mentors and protégés alike.

District-Sponsored Workshops and Seminars

Many school districts provide professional-development opportunities aimed at certain areas of focus: assessment, brain-based learning, and process management, to name a few. Mentors can work with protégés to choose that which best fits their situation. While staff development that is part of a schoolwide effort at improvement is infinitely more effective than relatively short individual seminars or workshops, new and veteran teachers can certainly benefit from quality staff-development sessions that engage them and model ways for them to engage their students. In the absence of an overall continuous-improvement model at the school level, these workshops and seminars may be helpful in providing strategies and ideas teachers can incorporate into an overall continuous-improvement strategy.

Visits With Teachers

Mentors can arrange for protégés to visit the classrooms of teachers inside or outside the district where formative assessments are used on a consistent basis. If there are teachers who use run charts to track student progress, or where students chart their own progress over time, visits to those classrooms would certainly be in order. Teachers who year after year show consistent improvement in state assessments might also be destinations where protégés could spend some time. As mentioned earlier, modeling is important, and any teacher whose students show relentless progress toward meeting goals and standards should have much to share with new teachers who understand better when they are able to visit a classroom, see something done, and then spend some time with the teacher who did it.

Role of Professional-Development Library

In Mr. Crandall's middle school, Trey, Shellie, and the other teachers had access to a well-developed professional-development library with books, journals, and computers for teacher use. Two volumes that would be of great use in any library dedicated to improvement within the schoolhouse are *The Handbook for SMART School Teams* and *The Power of SMART Goals* by Anne Conzemius and Jan O'Neill (2002; 2006), along with *Results: The Key to Continuous School Improvement and Results Now: How We Can Achieve Unprecedented Improvements in Teaching and Learning* by Mike Schmoker (1999; 2006). These books provide a framework for continuous improvement, including the PDSA (plan, do, study, act) cycle I outlined earlier in this chapter. Mentors should visit the library often with protégés; indeed, it could be the venue for meetings among small groups of teachers in the building.

Working on Feedback Mechanisms

Feedback is critical to success on the part of students, and mentors can explore with new teachers various ways of providing feedback that is effective. Putting check marks or letter grades on completed homework assignments, for example, does not give students anything in the way of meaningful feedback that would help them improve. After looking at several studies on the effect of feedback, Marzano, Pickering, and Pollock (2001) report that teachers should provide "students with an explanation of what they are doing that is correct and what they are doing that is not correct" (p. 96). Feedback, according to Marzano, Pickering, and Pollock, should be timely and "should reference a specific level of skill or knowledge" (p. 98). There are several good books on feedback, one of which is Susan Brookhart's (2008) *How to Give Effective Feedback to Your Students*. Another is *Checking for Understanding*, by Douglas Fisher and Nancy Frey (2007). Checklists and rubrics also provide students with a way to self-assess, and Kay Burke's (2006) *From Standards to Rubrics in 6 Steps: Tools for Assessing Student Learning, K–8* is another book mentors will want to have on hand in the professional-development library.

Final Thoughts

Mentors and protégés should often ask what is and is not working in their respective classrooms. This can be part of a larger discussion when all the mentors and new teachers get together, but it cannot be ignored. New teachers need to get into the habit of self-assessing and taking critical looks at their own instruction and process management. Teachers who do not commit to this approach early may *never* commit, and taking a systemic approach to self-assessment is critical in building the capacity for continuous improvement. If there is a schoolwide approach to steady improvement—so much the better. Either way, mentors need to help protégés develop the ability to consistently and relentlessly look at process and results in an effort to improve both.

In Chapter 8, we'll take a final look at how the school community can come together in support of new teachers. Those new teachers need to understand that in a business that is perhaps equal parts perspiration and inspiration, the latter should not be underestimated, and it should come from mentors, administrators, and colleagues throughout the building and school district.

8

Perspiration
and Inspiration

The path to master teacher is not an easy one. Novice teachers who are thrown into their own classrooms without an induction program to help them prepare will find the going tough. It is perhaps telling that the word most often used to describe the first few months of a teacher's career is *survival*. This is preceded by *anticipation* and succeeded in turn by *disillusionment, rejuvenation, reflection,* and—once more—by *anticipation* (Moir, 1999, as cited in Bartell, 2005, pp. 34–35). It seems to me that the first task of any induction program is to explain this predictable progression to teachers and then begin to provide experiences and understandings to better prepare teachers for the first days and weeks of teaching.

One way to do this is to move the reflection process up alongside anticipation. As we have said in earlier chapters, even novice teachers are veteran students. They have been in scores of classrooms from kindergarten through at least four years of college. Shellie was hired in the spring, and Trey, her mentor, wasted absolutely no time in seeing to it that she observed superb teachers in action. Periods of reflective conversation orchestrated by Trey and Mr. Crandall were aimed at surfacing insights from Shellie's own experience and depth of knowledge. Their support system kicked into gear the moment Shellie was hired, and reflection was part of the process from the beginning.

Another key element of the induction program was that Mr. Crandall, Trey, and everyone else in the middle school did not simply *tell* Shellie how she could become more successful as a new teacher. She observed good teachers in action and reflected on what she saw, what she heard, what she inferred—and then climbed the cognitive ladder to the application level. Trey, as her mentor, facilitated this formal inquiry process as Shellie began to think about what she observed in those several classrooms, *integrating all this with what she already knew in an attempt to create new understandings.*

All of which returns us to that big-picture view we spoke of earlier; what would working the plan of a powerful induction program look like if the seminal events within the system were laid out from end to end? In this final chapter, we'll suggest some possible steps to affecting student performance through thoughtful interventions on the part of administrators, mentors, and others in the leadership pipeline whose collective responsibility it is to welcome, train, and retain new teachers. Having implied a linear progression of events, however, it is worth pointing out that the components of a successful induction system do not simply hand off to one another as runners in a relay might hand off the baton and subsequently retire from the race to await its outcome. Components of a successful program are interconnected and interdependent. They keep coming back into the game, so to speak, to contribute again and again.

An example of this is the role of professional development in the continuous-improvement process of a new teacher. Professional development is not just something that happens only when a nationally known presenter comes to town; it is rather an ongoing process of workshops, individual and collaborative reflective practice, journal articles containing new ideas and interesting theories, classroom observations, book clubs, analyzing assessment data, informal conversations about what works in this or that teacher's classroom, and the observational evidence of a teacher's own eyes and ears as he or she assesses what works and does not work in the classroom. Professional development is ongoing, and it is most effective for teachers when it is tied to professional goals and results.

Before the new teacher comes on board, the school's leadership team needs to decide how it may choose to treat a novice teacher with virtually no experience or a veteran teacher new to the building. The induction system should take into account that whoever is hired to replace a retiring teacher is going to fit into one of these two categories. It is reasonable to expect that—novice or veteran—the school has expectations for its teachers that are in line with its basic beliefs and standards. This should be made clear to any veteran teachers applying for the position.

A veteran social studies teacher who has fallen into the lecture, video, worksheet, read-the-chapter-and-answer-the-questions-at-the-end cycle may not want to hear about pair share, movement in the classroom, or the many uses of formative assessments. If the principal and the leadership team have the ability to actually hire one teacher among many applicants, they should not be swayed by the fact that Mr. So-and-so has many years of experience. Observing the *kids* in the class of a veteran teacher will most likely tell members of the leadership team all they really need to know.

During the interview process, it should be made clear to prospective hires as to what their first two or three years will look like, and I have already said I believe new teachers should be in the classrooms of building-level and district-level teachers who exemplify the best in what the school is looking for when it comes to teacher replacements. Mentors or the leadership team charged with developing the induction program should seek out those who possess the nine qualities we examined in Chapter 1 and arrange with them for repeated visits by novice teachers.

As happened with Shellie, classroom visits should be arranged quickly, if possible before the old school year is out. For teachers hired during the summer, set up these visits once the new teachers have their procedures and routines in place. Letting new teachers observe the very best has always seemed to me to be a good use of the substitute teacher budget line. On the inclusion team of which I was a member in the early '90s, we often shifted personnel to accommodate absences for half a day or a full day without having to tap the budget. Covers can be provided if funds are not available. Frankly, anything that contributes to creating a healthy, happy teacher almost guarantees that teacher will use fewer sick days during the course of the year. Show me a largely dissatisfied faculty and I'll show you a high absentee rate among those unhappy campers.

Over my last several years in central office, I had the pleasure of working with teacher mentors as part of a districtwide mentor-training program. As part of the mentor-training workshops, we always asked about their most positive and negative experiences in their first year of teaching. We heard some amazing stories, and a general theme was one of support. Listening to those tales of first-year experiences, I was reminded of how much new teachers need the support of administrators, mentors, and colleagues during that sometimes-tentative entry into the profession. We heard stories of amazing teacher mentors, and we heard lamentable tales of schools that provided no support whatsoever, and for whom "Hang in there!"

seemed to be the sum total of the support mechanism provided from the top. Teacher mentors would do well to think back to their first year of teaching, an effort that might stir a good deal of empathetic understanding for the new teachers for whom they are responsible for one, two, or even three years.

The Value of Inspiration

Much in education is quantifiable. In fact, we should be looking at data, and collaborative teams can determine a great deal from the results they observe. Measuring is a natural part of chronicling growth. As we saw in Chapter 7, measured success can come through the use of a continuous-improvement cycle such as plan-do-study-act, where feedback and analysis play an important role in ensuring forward progress. Adding the time spent for an effective collaborative improvement process to the hours spent in the classroom is undoubtedly hard work. However, seeing students improve on a consistent basis is a key source of inspiration for the teachers who played a big role in facilitating that progress; we should not underestimate the power of inspiration in education.

Competence is a key factor in motivation. Deci (1995), in order to test this, conducted a simple experiment where two groups of people were given two puzzles to solve. Although the puzzles did not look any different on the surface, one was in fact more difficult. Those in the group that had the more difficult task did less well. "As expected," as reported by Deci, "those who received evidence of their own competence were subsequently more intrinsically motivated than those who saw evidence of relative incompetence" (pp. 66–67). Knowing I have demonstrated competence in a given task may be far more effective as a motivator than external praise. Concrete evidence of my own classroom competence (my students' steady progress in the area of writing skills, for example) has always been its own reward for me, and far more motivating than hearing "Good job!" from someone else.

Too many new teachers wait until the first week of school to consider just what is going to happen in the classroom. When this happens, novice teachers may remain in reactive mode for many weeks or months. In the same way, induction programs that wait until the first week teachers come back to kick into gear are not doing all they could do to build the new teacher's competence by giving him or her every advantage. For teachers hired late in the summer, a head start may not be possible, but in cases when contracts are signed in the spring or early summer, time is of the essence. As we saw in Chapter 5, planning is key for a novice teacher, *and mentors can facilitate this early planning*. The sooner new teachers can dig into their own body of knowledge and experience, assisted by an induction program, the more confident they may become.

If teachers are motivated by their own competence, along with the growing competence of their students, it follows that induction programs should do everything in their power to inspire the kind of confidence that will lead to competence. In order for disillusionment to take root for teachers, there has to be a sharp contrast between what they *thought* teaching would be like and the *reality* of it all three months into the school year. Inspiration, along with concrete tools for success, can come from mentors, colleagues, administrators, and support staff willing to spend the time necessary to increase the confidence and competence of new teachers. Mentors and administrators can inspire by being positive, enthusiastic, and competent themselves. Mostly, however, they can provide new teachers with a reflective capacity for improvement that will outlast the official novice teacher-induction time frame. The induction scaffold should be in place until, bit by bit, it is dismantled—to be replaced in turn by a confident and competent teacher practitioner who can solve problems on her own but also has come to value the collaborative model of mutual support and improvement reflected in the induction program.

We began this book by looking at qualities of highly effective teachers. Every new teacher can remember and talk about one or two great teachers in his or her K–12 experience. I have facilitated hundreds of such conversations, and in countless cases, new or would-be teachers credit these superb educators with their own desire to work with students. Teachers often tell these inspirational stories with great emotion, and it is clear after listening to them over the course of 15 years as a trainer that we should not underestimate the power of inspiration.

Teacher mentors can inspire by the sheer impact of their dedicated efforts on behalf of protégés. Administrators can inspire by relentlessly pursuing excellence in the building and by committing to a solid and well-managed continuous-improvement system that benefits everyone in the school community. Veteran teachers who are not part of the official mentoring process can nevertheless contribute to the ultimate success of someone new in their midst. Support staff can go out of their way to make certain that no new teacher has to worry about anything other than instruction. In Shellie's case, we saw that the custodians were more than willing to get Shellie's room ready first, along with the classrooms of the other three new teachers.

In Shellie's school, the continuous-improvement model walked hand in hand with the professional-development program; the professional-development program supported the induction process; and the induction process contained as a key component a very active and effective mentoring program. The mentoring program contributed directly to the professional growth of Shellie and the other three new teachers in the middle school. Most important, everything that happened in Mr. Crandall's schoolhouse directly and positively impacted the educational development of children.

Final Thoughts

Teaching may not be for the faint of heart, but it is for those *with* heart. It is also for those fully prepared to perspire and inspire, perhaps in equal measure. Teachers must be able to multitask in pursuit of performance excellence for themselves and for their students. In the first book in this trilogy, *The Active Classroom* (Nash, 2008), I compared the role of teachers to that of an orchestra conductor:

> The musicians make the music, but the conductor is in a position to influence the flow of the music, affecting, by her actions, the volume, tempo, and timing. She gives feedback when necessary and acknowledges effort constantly. A symphony is the ultimate collaborative effort. Everyone contributes. (p. xvi)

Teachers facilitate process, acknowledge effort, provide feedback, and by doing all this positively affect the outcome for the students in their care. Mentors must help new teachers understand their role and should provide multiple opportunities to observe and talk with those master teachers who, in the same way that great orchestra conductors demand excellence and develop talent, bring out the very best in their students.

If we begin with the end in mind, we come back to students who are well served by a system that would not exist were it not for them. They, too, are inspired by great teachers and administrators. They are inspired by custodians who take the time to read to them, and by cafeteria workers who take the time to talk to them and create relationships out of whole cloth. As it most certainly is with new teachers, students need to be confident of their growing competence in coursework that will assist them not just in school but also in the workplace and in life. We should not underestimate the power and influence of inspiration; it comes from within, it comes from without, and it should come often for our children and for the people who have made the decision to pursue our nation's noblest profession.

Epilogue

Near the end of Shellie's fourth year as a teacher, Trey celebrated the completion of his first year as an assistant principal at their middle school. Because of his outstanding work with new teachers over the past several years, Trey was asked by Mr. Crandall to take over leadership of the new teacher induction program. Trey and Mr. Crandall, along with the other assistant principal, the head custodian, the cafeteria manager, and three teacher leaders, constituted the continuous-improvement team for the middle school. This leadership cadre spent a great deal of time looking closely at issues directly affecting school climate and student performance. Faculty meetings were dedicated to looking at data (test results and surveys), reporting on books and articles, discussing what was and was not working in classrooms, and responding to suggestions from members of the school community gathered in expanded meetings that included parents. The mentor program was not a separate entity; it was interwoven into the overall improvement system at the middle school.

In May, Trey asked Shellie to meet with him in the professional-development library that was part of the school's media center. They met after school, and as soon as she arrived, Trey invited her to take a seat and poured them each a cup of coffee from the coffeemaker in the corner of the room. One entire wall was filled floor to ceiling with books devoted to teaching and learning, including several journals to which the school subscribed.

Trey handed Shellie a coffee mug and sat down next to her. After a minute or two of small talk, Trey got to the point, saying, "Shellie, Mr. Crandall and I are pleased with what you have accomplished in the last four years. Your students' test scores have improved each year, and the comments on the parent and student surveys are extraordinary. Also, your students and their parents consistently indicate their support for the way you run your classroom. The Cardinal team has really benefited from your first four years with them. Your team meetings are not about playing the blame game, and the whole team demonstrates a commitment to progress and forward movement."

"I appreciate that, Trey, and I can truly say that I enjoy teaching here, and I can also say that without the new-teacher induction program I might have done less well. My first year was hectic, but I concentrated on getting my procedural act together during the first month, something that made the rest of the year far less difficult than it might otherwise have been. Your mentorship was a big plus during my first two years here," said Shellie.

Trey nodded his thanks and said, "I had a great mentor in Mrs. Slattery, and my first year here was a distinct improvement over my very first year of teaching at a school where mentors were that in name only. That difficult first year gave me tremendous perspective when I moved to this school."

Shellie nodded. "My college roommate left teaching after one year because of a situation similar to yours."

Trey took a sip of coffee and said, "We have three new teachers coming on board this fall, Shellie, and Mr. Crandall and I would like you to become a teacher mentor. You already know we take that position seriously, and the school district has a two-day training program during the summer. Are you interested?"

With no hesitation, Shellie said, "I would enjoy that, Trey. Being a mentor here means having the support of administrators and colleagues, and the summer training will help."

"That's great," said Trey. He looked out the window of the professional-development library into the media center. "What elements of the induction program here helped you the most as a new teacher, Shellie?"

It was Shellie's turn to look out the window. Sipping some coffee, she replied, "First, I would say it was the effort you, Mr. Crandall, and my Cardinal teammates made to communicate with me right after I was hired in the spring. As I recall, you contacted me the day after I signed my contract and invited me to meet with you to discuss my new job. My college roommate heard nothing for weeks after she was hired. She did receive a call from her principal, but that was about it. She reported to school during the teachers' week and met everyone for the first time in a five-day information blitz she still describes as a total blur."

Trey nodded. "I know exactly how she felt. The contrast between my first year at the other school and my second year here could not have been more complete. What else helped you?"

Shellie paused and then smiled, saying, "You made it possible for me to see two great teachers in action shortly after I signed my contract. You also suggested I watch the kids and not the teachers in those classrooms as much as possible. I saw two classrooms where the kids were doing the work, while the teacher facilitated process. You had me reflect on what I saw and asked me questions. Those long reflective conversations helped me see what was possible for me."

Trey nodded again and said, "One thing we tend to forget is that even novice teachers are veteran students. They have had scores upon scores of teachers and professors by the time they graduate from college, and it is valuable to have them reflect on their own experiences as students. You may also recall that we had you reflect on your own teaching experiences as they unfolded over the course of two years."

"Yes," agreed Shellie, "and the reflection continues as part of the overall continuous-improvement process. There may be a formal end to the new-teacher induction process after a couple of years, but *reflection* and *improvement* are operational bywords at every turn in this school."

"Well, if you will accept the mentorship position, all our teacher mentors are meeting next week to begin planning for next year. Not everyone will have an immediate assignment, but we believe that teacher mentors improve their own performance as they continue to learn and reflect as part of the induction program."

Shellie smiled. "I accept, and I look forward to next week's meeting."

Seven years into her tenure at the middle school, Shellie had established a solid reputation as someone who expected and received much from her students. She was able to work as a mentor with a novice teacher for two years, and her protégé's evaluation of Shellie's interactions during that time was excellent. Shellie's classroom also became a frequent destination for new and experienced teachers who spent anywhere from a single class period to a full day with her. Shellie's students became used to seeing visitors, and they made it a point to greet each visiting teacher and show off their portfolios, grade run charts, and other evidence of their own considerable growth.

That spring the Director of Instruction from her district's central office approached Shellie about becoming an instructional coach at the middle school level—one of five such full-time coaches. She would work with social studies teachers at all middle school grade levels in a nonsupervisory capacity on an 11-month contract. Her job would be to model powerful engagement strategies, observe teachers, and work with the teacher mentors in those buildings. Shellie had accepted that position, and had been a district-level coach for three years when she learned from one of her old Cardinal teammates that Mr. Crandall would retire in the spring.

This retirement was sad news for staff members at the middle school, particularly those who had been with Mr. Crandall for his entire tenure as principal. Indeed, the entire school community was disappointed, but this bit of sad news was countered by the appointment of Trey as the new principal. Shellie attended the retirement party at Mrs. Slattery's home and spoke as one lucky enough to be nurtured in her first years of teaching in a system dedicated to her professional growth and development. She well understood the importance of that support.

Mr. Crandall's induction program would continue to function in his absence because of the years spent creating and refining it as part of a collaborative effort to improve instruction and, in a more general sense, create a place where students, teachers, and staff loved coming to school every day. His legacy included a mentoring program that trained and ultimately retained new teachers who never doubted for a moment the school's commitment to their success.

Appendix

Support From an Extended Family

Everyone in a new teacher's school community can—and should—feel compelled to invest in some way in that teacher's ultimate success. This investment, along with an effective start for a new teacher, will contribute to the continuous improvement efforts of the school and, by extension, the school district as a whole. Induction programs should be backed up with the resources that keep good teachers in the classroom. This effort should include teachers, administrators, and support staff dedicated to assisting and accelerating the growth of new teachers and teachers new to the school or district.

Increasingly, in the 21st century, Web access can provide virtually unlimited support possibilities for mentors and protégés alike. Help is just one mouse click away at any time of the day or night. Mentors, working with school- or district-level instructional technology personnel, can determine which Web sites might be of great value for new teachers. There are, for example, thousands upon thousands of lesson plans available to social studies teachers in every subject from geography to economics; this is true of every subject imaginable. Assuming there is a computer in a school's professional-development library; mentors can add some helpful sites to a list of Favorites for easy access later on. Instructional technology teachers can tag such sites in all subject areas for retrieval when new teachers—or all teachers—need access to ideas, lesson plans, or other content information.

In December, 2008, English teacher and author Jim Burke created *The English Companion Ning,* an online site dedicated to the support of English teachers (Rich, 2009). In just a few months there were almost 7,000 members from all over the world. Sites like this create virtually limitless social networking possibilities for teachers—new or otherwise—hungry for information and loaded with questions related to process and content. Such availability provides a mentor and her protégé rich fodder for reflective conversations that will benefit both. A mentor who knows she has been assigned a protégé for the coming year can take the time to search for the kind of Web-based destinations that will further support new teachers beyond the geography of building and district.

In larger districts where such sites can be located and vetted at the central-office level, instructional technology specialists can work indirectly with mentors—or directly with new teachers—to assist in building-level induction efforts. The Internet being what it is, the appropriateness of what can be accessed is always a concern. Well-planned 21st century induction programs should take into account that brand-new teachers fresh out of college are digital natives; the resources harnessed on their behalf need to take into account their tendency to connect via the Web. Building- and district-level personnel familiar with the rich sources of information and social-connectivity possibilities available on the web can make this part of the regular new-teacher induction program.

In Chapter 1, we looked at nine qualities superb teachers might possess, and throughout the book I have recommended that mentors provide protégés with opportunities to observer great teachers in action. Some districts have begun putting professional development opportunities online, and in many cases, that includes taping their best teachers so that others can observe the lessons at their own convenience. Any district that provides such snapshots of good instruction is contributing to the continuous-improvement process at every level. I would suggest that protégés not simply view video after video with no guidance or follow-up conversations. In a meeting prior to the viewing, mentors can discuss with protégés what they might look for as they view a particular lesson. The next day, mentor and protégé can meet for a few minutes to discuss what the protégé saw; indeed they might watch it again together in order to bring the perspective of the mentor into play. It may be that several new teachers can view the tape together, after which a mentor who has viewed it with them can facilitate a reflective conversation about what they saw and how what they saw can inform their own instructional practice.

While I believe these taped lessons can be extremely helpful for protégés, I suggest that they not totally replace personal visits to "live" classrooms. Viewing the lesson in real time and on-site allows the protégé to see not only the teacher, but the students as well. I have come to believe that watching students during a class period can often tell the observer more than watching the teacher. As we mentioned earlier in the book, protégés can use the opportunity of a classroom visit to look for signs of engagement and understanding on the part of students. Many a beautifully planned lesson has failed because of a lack of engagement and/or understanding on the part of the students for whom it was written. Once again, a follow-up conversation with a mentor can help provide perspective, deepen understanding, and inform instruction.

Those of us who are digital immigrants can remember a time when print sources provided most of our information about anything. For us, the wonder of global interconnectivity simply boggles the mind. The reality of this sort of extended family, available at the click of a mouse for new teachers today, shifts the role of the mentor more than ever to one of facilitator of process. A mentor unfamiliar with things Internet can seek assistance from a variety of sources within the school community; a school community dedicated to the success of its new teachers should respond willingly to these requests for help. New teachers who understand that the teachers, administrators, and staff around them are committed to their growth and development stand a better chance of succeeding in their chosen profession than those for whom support is visibly lacking.

District- and building-level leadership teams can best serve new teachers by being active in pursuit of resources—human and otherwise—that will assist in their growth. Key to all this is the direct involvement of the community of professionals at the building level. New teachers, along with teachers new to the school family, need to see support at every turn. The extended family includes central-office personnel and, increasingly in the 21st century, the myriad electronic connections available to new teachers day and night. School leadership teams that seek to *maximize the involvement of people and resources* will go a long way toward facilitating the continuous improvement journey of new teachers. This support may make the difference for new teachers who want to succeed in this noblest of professions.

References

Allen, R. H. (2010). *High-impact teaching strategies for the 'XYZ' era of education.* Boston: Pearson.

Bartell, C. A. (2005). *Cultivating high-quality teaching through induction and mentoring.* Thousand Oaks, CA: Corwin Press.

Bluestein, J. (2008). *The win-win classroom: A fresh and positive look at classroom management.* Thousand Oaks, CA: Corwin Press.

Bobek, B. L. (2001, September/October). Teacher resiliency: A key to career longevity. *The Clearing House, 75*(4), 202–205.

Bondy, E., & Ross, D. D. (2008, September). The teacher as a warm demander. *Educational Leadership, 66*(1), 54–62.

Bransford, J., Darling-Hammond, L., & LePage, P. (2005). Introduction. In L. Darling-Hammond & J. Bransford (Eds.), *Preparing teachers for a changing world: What teachers should learn and be able to do* (pp. 1–39). San Francisco: Jossey-Bass.

Brookhart, S. M. (2008). *How to give effective feedback to your students.* Alexandria, VA: Association for Supervision and Curriculum Development.

Burke, K. (2005). *How to assess authentic learning* (4th ed.). Thousand Oaks, CA: Corwin.

Burke, K. (2006). *From standards to rubrics in 6 steps: Tools for assessing student learning, K–8.* Thousand Oaks, CA: Corwin.

Conzemius, A., & O'Neill, J. (2002). *The handbook for SMART school teams.* Bloomington, IN: National Education Service.

Conzemius, A., & O'Neill, J. (2006). *The power of SMART goals: Using goals to improve student learning.* Bloomington, IN: Solution Tree.

Costa, A. (2008). The school as a home for the mind. Thousand Oaks, CA: Corwin.

Daresh, J. (2003). *Teachers mentoring teachers: A practical approach to helping new and experienced staff.* Thousand Oaks, CA: Corwin.

Deci, E. (1995). *Why we do what we do: Understanding self-motivation.* New York: Penguin.

Denton, P. (2008). The power of our words: Teacher language influences students' identities as learners. Five principles keep that influence positive. *Educational Leadership, 66*(1), 28–31.

Fisher, D., & Frey, N. (2007). *Checking for understanding: Formative assessment techniques for your classroom.* Alexandria, VA: Association for Supervision and Curriculum Development.

Goodlad, J. (2004). *A place called school* (2nd ed.). New York: McGraw-Hill.

Grissmer, D., & Kirby, S. N. (1997). Teacher turnover and teacher quality. *Teachers College Record, 99*(1), 45–56.

Haycock, K. (1998, Summer). Good teaching matters: How well-qualified teachers can close the gap. *Thinking K–16, 3*(2), 1–2.

Hord, S., & Sommers, W. A. (2008). *Leading professional learning communities: Voices from research and practice.* Thousand Oaks, CA: Corwin.

Ingersoll, R. M., & Smith, T. M. (2004, Fall). What are the effects of induction and mentoring on beginning teacher turnover? *American Educational Research Journal, 41*(3), 681–714.

Jackson, R. R. (2009). *Never work harder than your students & other principles of great teaching.* Alexandria, VA: Association for Supervision and Curriculum Development.

Jenkins, L. (2003). *Improving student learning: Applying Deming's quality principles in classrooms* (2nd ed.). Milwaukee, WI: American Society for Quality.

Jensen, E. (2004). *Brain compatible strategies.* San Diego, CA: The Brain Store.

Johnson, S. M., & Birkeland, S. (2003, Fall). The schools that teachers choose. *Educational Leadership, 60*(8), 20–24.

Jones, F. (2007). *Tools for teaching* (2nd ed.). Santa Cruz, CA: Fredric H. Jones & Associates.

Jonson, K. F. (2002). *Being an effective mentor: How to help beginning teachers succeed.* Thousand Oaks, CA: Corwin.

Kline, L., & Salzman, J. (2006). Mentoring: A serendipitous professional development opportunity. In J. R. Dangel (Ed.), *Research on teacher induction: Teacher education yearbook XIV* (pp. 169–192). Lanham, MD: Rowman & Littlefield Education.

Knight, J. (2007). *Instructional coaching: A partnership approach to improving instruction.* Thousand Oaks, CA: Corwin.

Lambert, L. (2003). *Leadership capacity for lasting school improvement.* Alexandria, VA: Association for Supervision and Curriculum Development.

Lezotte, L. (1992). *Creating the total quality effective school.* Okemos, MI: Effective Schools Products.

Lipton, L., & Wellman, B. (2004). *Data-driven dialogue: A facilitator's guide to collaborative inquiry.* Sherman, CT: Mira Via.

Lipton, L., & Wellman, B. (2005). Cultivating learning-focused relationships between mentors and their protégés. In H. Portner (Ed.), *Teacher mentoring and induction: The state of the art and beyond* (pp. 149–163). Thousand Oaks, CA: Corwin.

Marzano, R., Pickering, D., & Pollock, J. (2001). *Classroom instruction that works: Research-based strategies for increasing student achievement.* Alexandria, VA: Association for Supervision and Curriculum Development.

McCutcheon, R., & Lindsey, T. (2006). *It doesn't take a genius: Five truths to inspire success in every student.* New York: McGraw Hill.

Nash, R. (2008). *The active classroom: Practical strategies for involving students in the learning process.* Thousand Oaks, CA: Corwin.

Nash, R. (2010). *The active teacher: Practical strategies for maximizing teacher effectiveness.* Thousand Oaks, CA: Corwin.

Portner, H. (2005a). Embedding induction and mentoring into the school's culture. In H. Portner (Ed.), *Teacher mentoring and induction: The state of the art and beyond* (pp. 75–92). Thousand Oaks, CA: Corwin.

Portner, H. (Ed.). (2005b). *Teacher mentoring and induction: The state of the art and beyond.* Thousand Oaks, CA: Corwin.

Resta, V. (2006a). Overview and framework. In J. R. Dangel (Ed.), *Research on teacher induction: Teacher education yearbook XIV* (pp. 103–105). Lanham, MD: Rowman & Littlefield Education.

Resta, V. (2006b). Summary and conclusions. In J. R. Dangel (Ed.), *Research on teacher induction: Teacher education yearbook XIV* (pp. 193–200). Lanham, MD: Rowman & Littlefield Education.

Rich, E. (2009, October). The world's largest English department. *Teacher Professional Development Sourcebook, 2*(1), 26–29.

Rowley, J. (2005). Mentor teachers as instructional coaches. In H. Portner (Ed.), *Teacher mentoring and induction: The state of the art and beyond* (pp. 109–127). Thousand Oaks, CA: Corwin.

Schlechty, P. C. (2001). *Shaking up the schoolhouse: How to support and sustain educational innovation.* San Francisco: Jossey-Bass.

Schmoker, M. (1999). *Results: The key to continuous improvement* (2nd ed). Alexandria, VA: Association for Supervision and Curriculum Development.

Smith, A. (2005). *The brain's behind it: New knowledge about the brain and learning.* Norwalk, CT: Crown House.

Sweeny, B. (2002). Structures for induction and mentoring programs. In K. Burke (Ed), *Mentoring guidebook: Starting the journey* (pp. 5–29). Thousand Oaks, CA: Corwin.

Walsh, J. A., & Sattes, B. D. (2005). *Quality questioning: Research-based practice to engage every learner.* Thousand Oaks, CA: Corwin.

Westheimer, J. (2008). Learning among colleagues: Teacher community and the shared enterprise of education. In Cochran-Smith, M., Feiman-Nemser, S., & McIntyre, D. J. (Eds.). *Handbook of research on teacher education* (3rd ed., pp. 756–783). New York: Routledge, Taylor & Francis Group and the Association of Teacher Educators.

Whitaker, T. (2004). *What great teachers do differently: 14 things that matter most.* Larchmont, NY: Eye on Education.

Wong, H. K. (2005). New teacher induction: The foundation for comprehensive, coherent, and sustained professional development. In H. Portner, *Teacher mentoring and induction: The state of the art and beyond* (pp. 41–58). Thousand Oaks, CA: Corwin.

Wong, H. K., & Wong, R. (2005). *How to be an effective teacher: The first days of school.* Mountain View, CA: Harry K. Wong.

Yost, D. S. (2006, fall). Reflection and self-efficacy: Enhancing the retention of qualified teachers from a teacher education perspective. *Teacher Education Quarterly, 33*(4), 59–76.

Zmuda, A., Kuklis, R., & Kline, E. (2004). *Transforming schools: Creating a culture of continuous improvement.* Alexandria, VA: Association for Supervision and Curriculum Development.

Index

CORWIN

A SAGE Company

The Corwin logo—a raven striding across an open book—represents the union of courage and learning. Corwin is committed to improving education for all learners by publishing books and other professional development resources for those serving the field of PreK–12 education. By providing practical, hands-on materials, Corwin continues to carry out the promise of its motto: **"Helping Educators Do Their Work Better."**